BETWEEN
COASTS

BETWEEN COASTS

FROM KAIPARA TO KAWAU

David Bateman

ISBN 1-86953-442-5

TEXT Vaughan Yarwood
PHOTOGRAPHS see page 144
CAPTIONS Tracey Borgfeldt and Chris O'Brien

PRODUCTION Pages Literary Pursuits
COVER AND BOOK DESIGN Sue Attwood

Printed in Hong Kong by Colorcraft

Rodney District evolved from the courage and
tenacity of its early settlers. It will be moulded by the
environmental awareness of the generations to come.

This book captures the beauty and character of
Rodney District as we enter the new millennium.
Enjoy each page: as the story unfolds, enriching our
knowledge of the land between the Tasman and Pacific
coasts. Celebrate with us.

DOUG ARMSTRONG QSO JP
MAYOR, RODNEY DISTRICT

CONTENTS

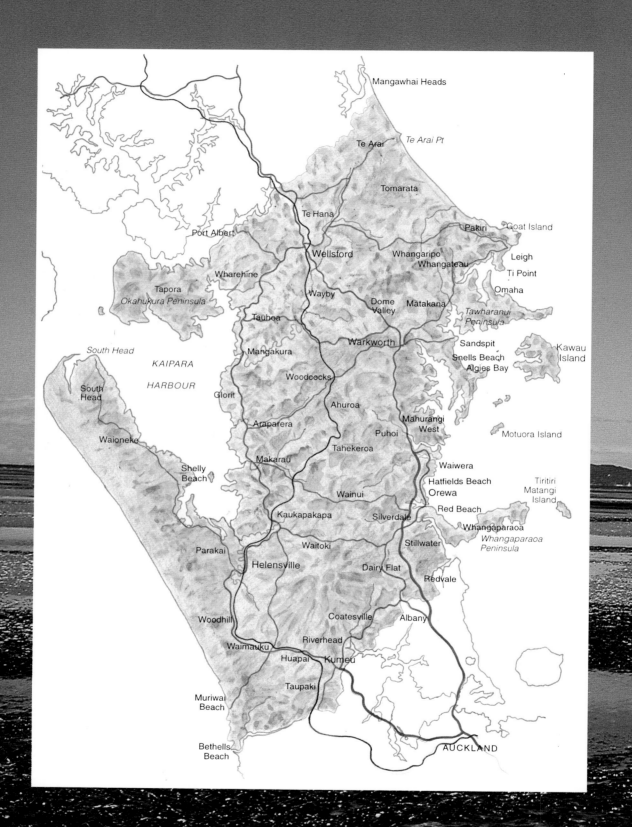

FOREWORD

*T*HE EVE OF A NEW MILLENNIUM is an excellent reason to commemorate the Rodney District, to look back and celebrate its achievements and to look forward to the challenges ahead.

The pioneers in these parts – sawyers, gumdiggers, farmers, road makers, railway workers and shipbuilders – recognised early on that the district we now know as Rodney was something special. After the initial plunder of its forests the land was cleared for farming and it has remained, essentially, a farming district. Its economy, however, has always been dependent on its coasts, its waterways and its proximity to Auckland.

Sir Gordon and Lady Mason

In the 1930s and 40s the Whangaparaoa Peninsula and east coast harbours became such popular holiday destinations that they were fondly known as 'the bachlands'. Many of those 'resorts' have become suburbs, but they still attract holidaymakers as well as permanent residents. In the last decade of the twentieth century Rodney was the fastest growing district in New Zealand. There are now more than 70,000 permanent residents, swollen by thousands over the summer holiday season as they come to enjoy the beauty of this magnificent coast and its rural hinterland.

Although I do not presume to qualify as a 'real' pioneer of Rodney I have lived here for over 70 years, run a business, farmed, and served on the council for 32 years – 16 as Rodney County chairman followed by three years as Rodney District's first Mayor. During this time I have observed momentous development and huge change.

While many of these changes have been significant, we have not seen the end of them. It is therefore critical to Rodney's future to plan carefully its development, protect the environment and ensure the District remains a great place in which to live, work and grow.

G. C. Mason

SIR GORDON MASON OBE JP

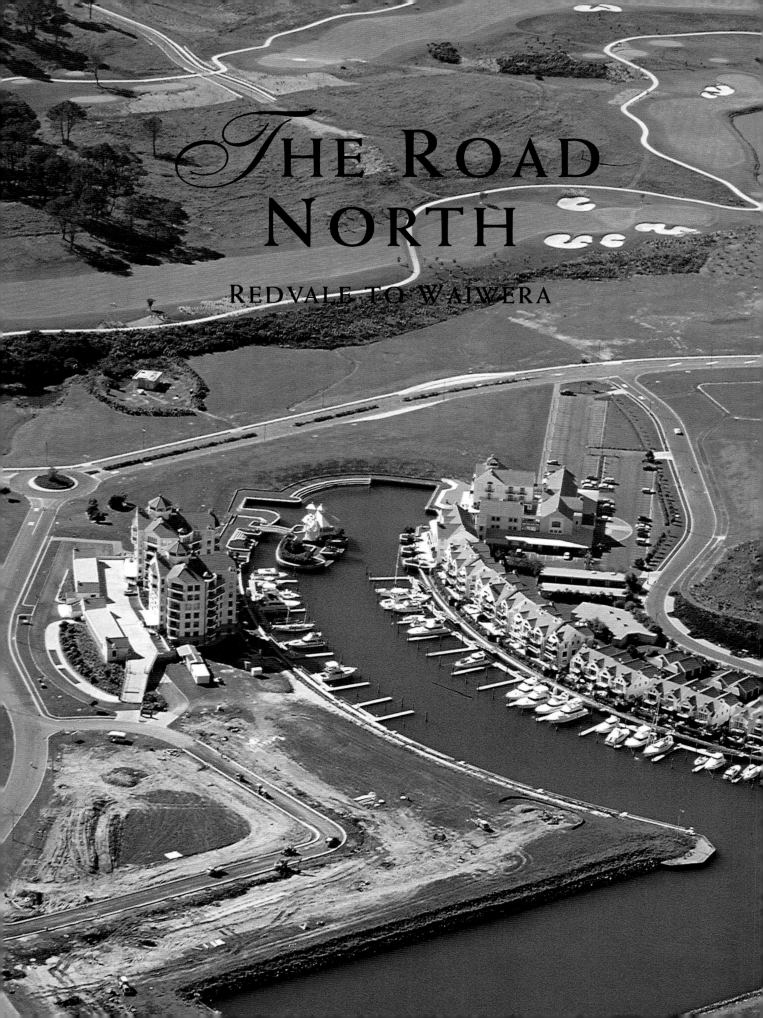

The Road North

Redvale to Waiwera

Development of Gulf Harbour on Whangaparaoa Peninsula began in the 1970s. Today it continues, with further canal-side apartments planned. Along with the Gulf Harbour Marina (below), it provides an ideal base for exploring the Hauraki Gulf by boat.

*R*odney District spans the North Auckland peninsula. To the west wild beaches of black sand and pounding surf screen the tranquil strands of the country's largest harbour – the Kaipara. To the east are spectacular coastlines, golden sands and the islands of the Hauraki Gulf. In between is a rural heartland steeped in history.

Cars struggled to negotiate the early roads around Rodney.
The winter of 1929, on the Ahuroa-Puhoi Road, was no exception.

A NEWSPAPER JOURNALIST, weighing up the prospects for Rodney District with its dairy farms and orchards, its winding rivers and indented bays, its diverse manufacturers and tourists' delights, concluded that to reach its potential, the region only needed 'the kiss of the prince of good roads'.

With Rodney on the verge of sustained growth, the time was right, the journalist urged, 'to come along and get in while the prices are right'.

Fair comment. But anyone acting on the advice when it was hot off the press would not thank the *New Zealand Herald*. Not that they are likely to be around to argue the point, given that the advice was offered in its pages some three-quarters of a century ago – 11 April 1923, to be exact.

Apart from the district's enduring natural beauty – Pakiri after an easterly blow, say, or the Kaipara's Shelly Beach in the stillness of dawn – little of what the *Herald* thought worth mentioning proved durable. Within a few years, the Port Albert apples it praised, grown around the Oruawharo River and 'known all over the world', had fallen victim to low prices and disease, and many of the orchards were ripped out. Port Albert itself had already been pushed into the commercial shade of nearby Wellsford and its butter factory was an early casualty. Likewise, Kaipara Flats refused to 'increase in importance' as predicted, despite its position on the lengthening rail line north.

Helensville, once one of the country's busiest ports, declined further as the trade in timber and kauri gum that had buoyed it continued to recede like the Kaipara tide. And Warkworth, that quiet English retreat for city-weary business people, remained at best – which meant in the good motoring months of summer – a stubborn three hours distant from Auckland. As with many settlements in the district early this century, Warkworth was slow to get all-weather access. The prince of good roads was often occupied elsewhere.

To reach its potential, the region only needed 'the kiss of the prince of good roads'

LEFT: The first stage of the new motorway north opening up the eastern side of Rodney District. The East Coast Road is the thin band to the right of the four-lane highway pushing through to Silverdale.

BELOW: The gently rolling landscape of Dairy Flat (bottom) is being transformed to accommodate the new road north. The whole project, spread over a distance of 27 km, requires some six million cubic metres of rock and soil to be shifted.

BELOW: Red Beach in the 1920s, when Whangaparaoa Peninsula was mostly farmland and baches.

BOTTOM: Like much of the peninsula beyond, Red Beach has succumbed to the unstoppable advance of suburban development.

Soon the whole coast was echoing to the sound of builders' hammers as suburbs spread over farmland and houses crept up on baches

Nevertheless, though commercial life flourished and died in Rodney, with new industries building on the ashes of the old, and with first one community then another brightening to prominence, development continued. The huge kauri forests from which villas and schooners, apple boxes and varnish resin were made, had gone, and the spade had turned over the barren gumlands for the last time. But dairying and plantation forestry gradually took their place, along with deer farms and specialised horticultural crops. Equally important, the continued growth of Auckland began to push business and financial services over the new harbour bridge as far north as Albany, and it pushed people even further. Soon the whole coast was echoing to the sound of builders' hammers as suburbs spread over farmland and houses crept up on baches, hounding them even in their secluded heartland on the Whangaparaoa Peninsula.

Reading the warning signs, planners began working on more effective road access to Puhoi and beyond as early as the 1960s. Feasibility studies were done, land was bought, environmental impact assessments were made and all the myriad hoops of due process were gone through until, in early 1997, the first heavy machinery was brought to bear on the green fields of Albany. Work on the largest single roading project in the country's history had begun.

It is called ALPURT, one of those charmless acronyms that massive construction projects seem to attract. Given that they often roll out over the landscape like forces of nature, it might be better if dams and motorways and land reclamation schemes were named the way tropical storms are – after people. The northern motorway extension project (Highway 'Betty', as it might be) is officially the Albany to Puhoi realignment – hence, ALPURT.

When finished in 2003, this 27-km stretch of highway will have cost an estimated $200 million, according to Laurie Taylor of Serco Consultancy, the project manager appointed by Transit New Zealand. In the process almost six million cubic metres of earth will have been shifted, seven interchanges made and 13 road and river crossings built.

The project is so big that it has been divided into two stages: the first comprises a four-lane extension of the present motorway just south of Albany Village and taking it on to Silverdale; the second links Silverdale with Puhoi and in the process tapers it to a two-lane expressway. Rodney District Council, meanwhile, is working on a link road to provide easy access to the motorway from Orewa.

FROM TOP: The busy marina at Gulf Harbour; part of the spectacular and challenging Gulf Harbour Country Club golf course; John Daly beating the bunkers during the 1998 World Cup of Golf; and the eventual winners – the English team of Nick Faldo and David Carter; Gulf Harbour town centre.

The 1998 World Cup of Golf, hosted by the Gulf Harbour Country Club, focused the attention of golfers around the world on the Whangaparaoa Peninsula.

MARINA LIFE
Gulf Harbour

THE INTERNATIONAL-STANDARD 6.4-km course was created by American designer Robert Trent Jones Jr to take advantage of what he called the site's 'magnificent topography'. The result is a par 72 course where, aside from engineered difficulties, competitors must constantly fight the distraction of panoramic gulf views.

The $25 million country club is part of an ambitious project called Gulf Harbour. Now in Singaporean ownership, this development, complete with canalside apartments, restaurants, shops, and conference centre, attempts to introduce a European ambience to what is one of the southern hemisphere's largest marinas.

With all 969 marina berths occupied and with a planned resident population of up to 9000 people, Gulf Harbour, begun in the 1970s, signals a new lifestyle direction on the Whangaparaoa Peninsula.

Benefits of the scheme will include reduced congestion in Orewa and Albany, a trimming of travel time from Puhoi to Albany of up to 15 minutes, and improved traffic safety compared to the dangerous, poorly aligned route which presently chalks up accident statistics 30 per cent above the national average. Also in the wind is a controversial toll road from Stanmore Bay on the Whangaparaoa Peninsula across the Weiti River near Stillwater to the new motorway at Redvale.

The impact of ALPURT is already being felt on the Hibiscus Coast and beyond, with some signs of house prices rising in anticipation of the Orewa link road and the new Weiti bridge: several new property developments are on the books.

Businesses in Rodney District stand to benefit from improvements in the flow of goods and services and from better access to labour and customers. Trucking companies from as far north as Whangarei anticipate more straightforward journeys to and from Auckland and realtors suggest that even more central city businesses will move north.

When stage one of the realignment is completed Silverdale will be spoilt for roading choice, with three major routes connecting it to the wider world: the motorway (the new State Highway One), the old highway and East Coast Road. Local businesses in Orewa, meanwhile, are looking forward to the completion of stage two which, by diverting through-traffic from the town's main street, should help reconnect the shops with the fine three-kilometre beach and the splendid views of islands in the Hauraki Gulf. That, at least, is the hope of local chemist Des Adams, chair of Destination Orewa. Adams would like to see Orewa regain its status as a beach resort destination, similar to Noosa in Queensland. He is encouraged by Warkworth's success in revitalising its shopping heart once through-traffic bypassed the town. The diversion will also be good news to local Lions and Rotary groups who have begun work on a new project, the Orewa Millennium Walkway, which meanders over eight kilometres along the foreshore and through several of the town's parks and reserves.

It could be said then, that with ALPURT, the prince of good roads has given Rodney not merely a belated kiss but something of a bearhug. The local roads are, however, quite another matter. With about 883 km of its 1633 km network still unsealed, Rodney District Council is fighting a battle of attrition to get blacktop out to the farm gates. In 1999 it set aside $27 million on road upkeep – around 43 per cent of its total maintenance budget – and $34 million on upgrading existing roads and providing new ones. The likely cost of upgrading over the next 20 years has been put at over $300 million. And, even if all goes according to plan, when the district arrives at the year 2020 it will still have around 700 km of unsealed road in tow.

LEFT: The Weiti Boating Club on the Whangaparaoa side of the Weiti (or Wade) River looks across to the settlement of Stillwater The proposed Weiti toll bridge will link the two and offer another route from the peninsula to the East Coast Road.

FAR LEFT: Until the new motorway is completed, the main road north passes through Silverdale, splitting the retail and light industrial estates.

TOP AND ABOVE: The Okura Walkway joins the Okura River estuary with Stillwater. The track climbs through luxuriant nikau-taraire-puriri forest and descends through stands of maturing kauri before hugging the coastline to Karepiro Bay and the Weiti River. Midway is the restored Dacre Cottage, built in the 1850s by a seafaring captain.

OUT OF THE GLASS CASE
Tiritiri Matangi

Four kilometres off the Whangaparaoa Peninsula lies the small island of Tiritiri Matangi, home to a unique experiment in conservation. For 10 years from 1984 spade-wielding school parties, community groups and individuals boarded charter boats and private craft to spend a day planting native trees on the island's grassy slopes.

OW, 250,000 POHUTUKAWA, flax, whau, mahoe, puriri and taraire later, the DoC-administered revegetation programme is almost complete. With plentiful food available the local birds, including bellbird, tui and kereru, are flourishing, along with introduced North Island robin, red-crowned parakeet, brown teal, little spotted kiwi, stitchbird, kokako and other endangered natives. The island supports some 10 per cent of the country's takahe population and so many saddlebacks – more than 600 from the original 20 pairs – that they are being 'exported' to other scientific reserves. Nowhere else can so many rare species be seen so readily in their natural environment.

Thanks to financial benefactors and the toil of countless gumbooted volunteers of all ages 'Tiri', as it is affectionately called, has become the country's most successful public-supported restoration programme, with 20,000 visitors a year stepping ashore to wander among the open sanctuary's threatened birds.

Evidence of early human occupation is not hard to find either. Nearby shark-fishing grounds attracted Maori to the island and reminders of those days include kumara storage pits, terraces, several pa and, until its removal in 1993, the surviving population of kiore.

The recent European past is even more in evidence underfoot, with the grazing land that until 1971 supported sheep and cattle still recognisable amid the regenerating forest.

Most visitors to the island at some point find themselves heading up the wharf road to Tiri's most famous landmark, perched on cliffs 85 m above the sea: its ironplated lighthouse (left).

The focal point of New Zealand's best preserved lighthouse complex, which includes fog horns, two keeper's cottages and a signal station, the 20-m-high lighthouse itself first shone in December 1864 and has been guiding Hauraki Gulf shipping ever since.

Powered by whale oil to begin with, then kerosene, the lighthouse was converted to acetylene in 1925 and thirty years later it was electrified. In 1956 an 11 million candlepower lamp was donated, giving Tiritiri Matangi the most powerful beam in the southern hemisphere. When it was automated for the second time in 1984 a smaller, less powerful quartz iodine lamp was installed.

Ferries regularly leave for the island from Auckland and Gulf Harbour on nearby Whangaparaoa Peninsula.

To experience the birdlife on Tiri is to gain some sense of the richness of New Zealand's forests before the arrival of Europeans. The birdsong strikes visitors as soon as they step onto the wharf. Just some of the rare birds likely to be seen on Tiri are, from top: stitchbird; takahe, seen here feeding a chick; and saddleback. Little blue penguins also nest and breed on the island.

RIGHT: Walking tracks provide easy access all over Tiri, including the more rugged east coast (opposite) with its picturesque coves and cliffs.

Greater Auckland, of which Rodney is a part, has the country's biggest regional economy – worth around $33 billion, or 34 per cent of the national total, in 1998. Since 1994, it has also been the country's fastest growing regional economy and has made something of a shift from manufacturing to financial services, transport and communications. Rodney itself is still largely agricultural, but the ranks of its 75,000 or so residents are increasingly being enlarged by commuters – the city-weary business people of the *New Zealand Herald* article. Which leaves Rodney at something of a turning point, with new arrivals – especially on the east coast – in danger of eroding the very things that attracted them north in the first place. So, former Council policy planning manager, Shane Hartley, a Whangaparaoa resident since the early 1980s, has a twinge of regret when he remembers hearing native birds while walking on the turf of a pony club at isolated Hobbs Bay. Now the site forms the entrance to the flamboyant Gulf Harbour marina.

An Act of Parliament in 1977 gave ownership of the seabed at Gulf Harbour to the Council, which then granted a licence for it to be developed as a marina, and horses made way for boats. Such a thing could not so readily be done in the current climate of resource management, but the very scale of Gulf Harbour, and other property projects like Pacific Plaza, has given momentum to settlement on the peninsula. The pace continues to quicken despite the Council's efforts to channel residential development away from the peninsula and into west Orewa and north Silverdale.

This rapid development has also increased the strain on roads and services on the peninsula, with international sporting events such as the recent World Cup of Golf and the America's Cup worsening the situation. The proposed Weiti Bridge crossing is an attempt at handling traffic growth that is predicted to reach 26,000 vehicles a day by 2002.

The plan has upset people like former dairy farmer Maureen Fullerton who, with her husband, runs Cedar Farm, a bed and breakfast at Stanmore Bay. The neighbouring property has been bought from its owner, the English writer Jeffrey Archer, for an intended new road servicing the route and, in her view, threatens the tranquillity her guests have come to enjoy on the 4-ha property. Such fallout is perhaps inevitable when a coastline known for its natural beauty experiences Rodney's rocketing growth.

Lifestyle changes in Rodney can be glimpsed from State Highway 18 which skirts a plantation forest near Riverhead. In Coatesville, amid signs for pick-your-own fruit and vegetables, are a scattering of lavish homesteads, some with elaborate artificial lakes and even aviaries. With their sweeping drives, spreading trees and generous floor plans, these properties are an index to Wainui's new money.

ABOVE: The charm of a rural landscape coupled with its proximity to Auckland has beckoned lifestylers to the tranquil vales of Wainui. Here in Coatesville, grand houses on 4-ha blocks, often with a lake in front, pasture, crops or flowers behind, are evidence of a burgeoning wealth.

LEFT, RIGHT AND INSET: Dairy Flat is an area of increasing horticultural diversity, with recent ventures into emu and deer husbandry mixing well with organic farming, forestry and floriculture.

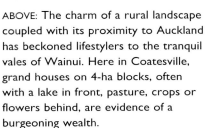

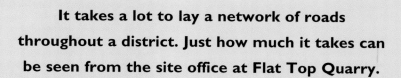

It takes a lot to lay a network of roads throughout a district. Just how much it takes can be seen from the site office at Flat Top Quarry.

ROCKS OF AGES
Flat Top Quarry

O N AN INSIDE WALL OF THE BUILDING is an old photograph taken in 1956 when quarrying had been going some 11 years. Flat Top then was just what its name implies — a big blunt trilby of a hill with hardly a scrap of vegetation on it.

Now, workers toil at the rock face 120 m below that old crown, all the intervening rock having been long since ground up and used for bulk fill or spread on roads up to 40 km away. Orders for aggregate are still heavy, with up to 235 truckloads a day being carried out, much of it earmarked for the new motorway.

In early 1999 a $5 million computer-controlled crushing plant, one of the country's first and capable of processing 860,000 tonnes a year, was installed to help keep up with demand. Quarry manager Phil Trafford says the site is nowhere near exhausted, and that it may prove possible to extract usable rock up to 200 m below ground level.

On the hill's crest middens were discovered — evidence, it is said, of the shellfish laboriously brought here from the Kaipara Harbour in pre-European times. In those days Flat Top was one of the highest points in Rodney and was plainly visible from Auckland.

It seems paradoxical that in order to build the roads to get here, the land that could most readily be seen had to go.

Quarrying started at Flat Top in the mid-1940s when it dominated the Wainui skyline and looked down on all its neighbours. Today it looks up at those same hills, decapitated after half a century of continuous quarrying. Since the installation of computer technology in 1998, 700 tonnes of basaltic andesite is processed every hour — a stark contrast to the physical efforts required at Wainui's first quarry at Stony Creek in the 1930s (above). The quarry is also used for the fiery destruction of Customs-seized and unlawful fireworks (below).

But a more subtle insight into the pressures on the rural way of life can be got further north, on the winding Haruru Road near Flat Top Quarry. Here, on a high terrace to the right, stands an impressive stadium-sized building signposted as Kelly Park Equestrian Centre. Owner June Thompson built the enclosed 86 m by 44 m arena five years ago, using money from the sale of nearby farmland. Incorporating shops, stables, a cafeteria and mezzanine viewing area, the $1.5-million building is the fruition of a life that has revolved around horses.

For nearly 30 years June farmed the land hereabouts, but when her marriage ended she took a gamble and financed the equestrian centre, named in memory of her daughter. She now runs 100 or so horses on the 360 ha that remain, having got rid of the farm stock.

'I don't think there is a farm round here that has made money in the past few years', she says. 'Rodney is losing about six dairy farms a year. Our best land is going under houses.'

The good land, she admits, is mostly to be found further north, around Wellsford and Warkworth. Down here the limestone country is puggy and full of tomos – dips or concealed holes that can be death to stock. June loses one or two horses a year to them and says it is not unknown to come across 10 or 15 sheep in a long line underground.

With farming so marginal an exercise here, it isn't surprising that much of the land out toward the east coast has been approved for subdivision into 'lifestyle blocks' – smaller than the traditional 4-ha blocks and more manageable for city folk bent on country living.

The upshot is that life has become dangerous for kids on ponies. The Council has no more spare land for pony clubs and some of the existing ones – like that at Hobbs Bay – have been pushed out. Horse lovers in Albany, which once had 14 clubs, are having to hitch their animals and move further out beyond the tide of suburban expansion. Now, Henderson has introduced a $200 fine for riding on the verge. And the motorists with no rural upbringing, increasingly common in these parts, often fail to make allowances for horses on the road.

June knows of several children killed while riding ponies. Indeed, that was one of the main motives for building the equestrian centre – to provide a space where young riders and others could enjoy their sport in safety. At the outset, there were plans to use the arena part time for other sports to subsidise the riding, but as it turned out they weren't necessary. The place is so popular that people come from as far as Howick to ride their horses, which can be grazed at Kelly Park, and show jumping can be held throughout the winter. The only difficulty June has is getting staff. 'Once there were a lot of country kids keen to work with horses. Now all they want to do is get to the city and party.'

ABOVE: A picturesque reminder of Wainui's rural heritage remains with the Waitoki windmill on Wainui Road.

BELOW: Changing rural scenes are provided by the Kelly Park Equestrian Centre, where horses and riders enjoy a top-class sporting facility that attracts horse lovers from all over Auckland.

If Kelly Park Equestrian Centre is tailored to horse lovers, the Hopper brothers hope to realise an equally ambitious lifestyle dream at Dairy Flat — an airfield park for people keen to take off from home. The plan calls for a development with 75 house lots, each with its own access to the runway.

In some ways this is a natural evolution from the successful Gulf Harbour on the Whangaparaoa Peninsula, where many of the houses have canal mooring literally at the back gate for yacht and powerboat owners, and others overlook the world-class 18-hole golf course. Rodney's growing population may be putting pressure on resources as well as stimulating unusual lifestyle responses, but some infrastructure projects in the district suggest that, with a little care, the environment can be safeguarded.

A few kilometres out of Dairy Flat, down the access road to the Redvale Lime quarry and past the North Harbour Trotting and Country Club, is Redvale Landfill, 69 ha of scooped and graded farmland fringed with trees. Described as the most comprehensively engineered land disposal site in the country, it has a refuse capacity of 10 million tonnes and a design life of 30 years. The first of its type to fully comply with the Resource Management Act, it won the Institute of Professional Engineers environment award in 1994, the year after it opened.

Landfill manager Chris Wills of Waste Management says Redvale will be a zero-discharge site by the end of the year. Nothing that is put there, in other words, will get out again, either by air or through leaching. One reason for that confidence is the geology of the place. It sits on a 100-m-thick pan of low permeability limerock and mudstone and is not above any significant aquifers. The parent company WMX Technologies is the world's largest environmental services company and, geologically, Redvale is one of its top three sites worldwide.

Equally impressive are plans to build a plant to generate electricity from gas produced by the decay of wastes. Currently this gas is just flared, but within 20 years, says Wills, Redvale could be pushing 20 megawatts back into the national grid.

In 2020 or so, once earth has been bulldozed over the last load of compacted waste, Redvale will be transformed into a (somewhat elevated) recreational reserve, what Wills calls 'North Shore's Cornwall Park'. Among the activities he would like to see develop there — equestrian events.

Europeans have been making a living from Wainui's soil since they first arrived.

TOP: Gumdigging was an important industry for Dairy Flat last century. One key site was Poyntons, near what are now Potters and Kennedy roads.

ABOVE: This dwelling was the home of a gumdigger called Birmingham and was situated just above the creek on Richards Road. As the gum ran out, the land was left to the new settlers to break in for farming.

Infrastructure projects in the district suggest that, with a little care, the environment can be safeguarded

LEFT: The Redvale Lime Company was started by the Dury family in the 1930s and has been churning out limerock and road metal ever since. Nowadays almost half a million tonnes is extracted each year, distributed throughout the region by a continuous coming and going of some 30 trucks and trailers. Redvale's neighbour, Waste Management, is gradually refilling and landscaping the exhausted part of the quarry's 38-ha site as demand increases for the disposal of waste.

BELOW: A misty morning at Dairy Flat — a far cry from the churned and pitted landscape left by the gumdiggers.

The Pioneer Village at Silverdale is run by the Wainui Historical Society and gives visitors a fascinating glimpse of the history of European settlement in the region. Many historic buildings form the nucleus of the Village, among them the Methodist Chapel (1860), a school (1878) and a parsonage (1887).

Thanks, then, to old friends like Kelly Park and unlikely new ones like Redvale, horses may have a future in Rodney. They undoubtedly had an important past. A good place to get a feel for the times when horse was king, surprisingly, is Silverdale or the Wade as it was known until 1850. In those days most settlers arrived by way of the Weiti River. Like other rivers hereabouts, the Weiti was first used to get at the kauri, and the Wade developed into one of the region's most active timber milling centres and a thriving port.

With the surrounding forest cleared, gumdiggers descended on the Wade for a time, then fruit trees were planted and the clay soil was sown in grass for sheep and cattle. Even today, the river has not been allowed entirely to take retirement, and barges from the Firth of Thames still navigate its course laden with gravel and sand.

For reasons best known to itself, Silverdale these days is noted for its factory shops and for the light industry that has grown up on its old gumlands. The eye-catching murals on one of the shops evokes the flavour of the area's settler past, which can be more authentically experienced by strolling a few hundred metres along Silverdale Street to the historic Pioneer Village.

LEFT: Dairy Flat's old Post Office, shifted into the Pioneer Village in 1999, served as a general store-cum-postal centre before the advent of the Rural Delivery Service in the early 1950s.

BELOW: Scenes from Silverdale's colourful past. The main coach crossing the Silverdale bridge in the 1890s; traffic hazards were a perennial problem on Wainui roads.

Here, on a small reserve beside the old Silverdale school (1878), are a cluster of colonial buildings relocated by volunteers of the hardworking Wainui Historical Society. Among them is a Methodist Parsonage (1887), from whose sheltered verandah a worn path leads to a herb garden tended by the Pioneer Herb Society.

One of the village's most interesting buildings is a Wesleyan Chapel. Built in Parnell about 1845 and transported here by sea some 11 years later, it is one of the country's oldest surviving churches. Nearby is a small museum of settler artefacts from the Hibiscus Coast. A gumdigger's whare, a bushman's shanty and a saw pit are reminders of the industries that once sustained the Wade, as Silverdale was first called, after Te Weiti, the Maori name for its river.

Across State Highway One, which drives a brutish wedge through Silverdale, is the Wade Hotel, largely unchanged from the days when travellers took advantage of proprietor Maurice Kelly's hospitality to break their journey. Kelly built the hotel in 1880 to replace one destroyed that year by fire. Early the next year, following completion of the East Coast Road, a mail coach service began running three times a week between Auckland and Waiwera, complementing the twice-weekly steamer service.

Then, as now, people had pressing reasons for getting up the coast.

BELOW LEFT: The landing at the Silverdale depot for the New Zealand Co-op Dairy Co Ltd in the 1920s.

BELOW: The exterior of the famous Wade Hotel, seen here in the early 1900s, has remained largely unchanged, though travellers may have a little trouble finding it in the Silverdale Industrial Estate.

MAIN PICTURE: The end of Whangaparaoa Peninsula looking back past Shakespear Regional Park and the army base.

ABOVE LEFT: The Hibiscus Coast is spoiled for choice when it comes to beaches. Above is the south end of Orewa Beach, a mecca for walkers and waders year-round.

ABOVE RIGHT: On the south side of the Peninsula is Arkles Bay. Whichever way the wind if blowing, it is possible to find a sheltered spot somewhere on Whangaparaoa.

ABOVE LEFT AND RIGHT: For the more adventurous, there are plenty of high-energy watersports happening throughout the year on the Hibiscus Coast.

The spit at Waiwera almost cuts right across the entrance to the Waiwera River, providing shelter for the estuary and mangroves.

VISITING
'THE DOCTOR'
Waiwera Hot Springs

In 1842, while sheltering from a storm at Waiwera, Scottish entrepreneur Robert Graham noticed Maori soaking in hot pools they had dug on the beach. They were Ngati Rangi, a powerful Thames tribe who visited the coast in large numbers to catch and preserve the plentiful dogfish and sharks, and to enjoy the natural springs.

BELOW: An earlier view of Waiwera
looking along the spit and across to
Wenderholm Regional Park. The bridge
and main road north can be seen top left.
Below that is the impressive hotel (c. 1907)
where visitors could relax and 'take the
waters'. And they are still doing it today.
Sadly, the hotel burned down in 1939.

ALEC HATFIELD, WHO GAVE HIS NAME to nearby Hatfields Beach, is
credited with being the first Pakeha to try the waters, but it was the
astute Graham who recognised the potential of the springs, known by Maori
as Te Rata – 'the doctor'. Someone called Johnson told him that after bathing
in the waters he was miraculously cured of a painful skin disease that had
plagued him for 16 years. Won over by the story, Graham set about buying
land at Waiwera, and in 1848 he opened a 'house for the accommodation of
invalids, travellers and pleasure parties'. It was part of New
Zealand's first spa and tourist facility.

The miracles kept happening. Typical was the case of an English
business owner named Thornton, a cripple who, for 15 years,
had got about on crutches. Wiesbaden and other European
spas had done nothing for him but after a six-week residence
at Waiwera he pronounced himself cured, threw away his
crutches and walked the 38 km to Auckland through bush.

Publicity doesn't get much better than that and by 1875 the
'strange chemical laboratories of Nature' were being touted
internationally. To satisfy demand Graham added 50 more
bedrooms to his establishment, and for good measure he
barged in several cottages and an entire hotel from Tararu
near Thames. Guests arrived in similar fashion. One visitor in
1882 wrote: 'At present the method is for the steamer to run
in as near shore as possible, cast anchor, and send her
passengers and cargo off in boats. The boats, in turn, run as
near the shore as is possible for them, and are met by a horse
and cart. It was the first time I had been at sea in a carriage
and the sensation was unique.'

That particular adventure was tamed in 1905 when a 400-m
wharf was built, and with its peacocks, croquet lawns,
bowling green, tennis courts, and formal gardens, Waiwera
spa achieved a distinctly European air.

All that suddenly came to an end in 1939 when the kauri hotel burned down
in a blaze that could be seen from Auckland's waterfront.

Today, artesian bores capture all the heated water before it reaches the beach,
but with its pools, spas and bottled mineral water the modern Waiwera
Thermal Resort ministers to weary bodies in a way Robert Graham would
have approved of.

After a six-week residence at Waiwera Thornton pronounced himself cured, threw away his crutches and walked the 38 km to Auckland through bush

INTO THE HEARTLAND

WAIWERA TO WARKWORTH

Beagles, horses and riders enjoy the hunt on a sunny day in rolling country around Warkworth.

BELOW: If watersport is preferred, take a paddle upriver from Wenderholm, winding through mangroves and farmland up to Puhoi.

North of the Hibiscus Coast suburban development gives way to a more rural landscape: here the hills are bigger, the roads fewer, the sea never very far away. Rivers and harbours cut deeply into sheep and cattle country, a land once clothed by the mighty kauri, now increasingly redressed in *Pinus radiata*. But the bush is making a comeback.

I N THE 1850s IT WAS A SETTLER COAST. From the Okura River to the Mahurangi and beyond, boats bearing immigrants nosed their prows into the tidal mouths, delivering the newcomers and their meagre tools of survival to the extensively forested land beyond the mangroves.

Before them had been the occasional American whalers, driven to shelter or drawn by the need to reprovision. Then came the ships with a mission, like HMS *Buffalo*, which sailed into Mahurangi Harbour in 1834 to load kauri spars.

Richard Hodgskin, purser's steward aboard the *Buffalo*, left his impressions of the ship's first visit to that 'lonely and romantic' harbour. 'While lying here, it blew as heavy a gale of wind, perhaps, as ever was remembered in New Zealand... but we rode it out in perfect safety,' he wrote. 'Notwithstanding the country is liable to heavy gales of wind, their effects are not so disastrous as might be imagined; for numerous whale ships are at all seasons of the year upon the coast, and the loss of one of them is indeed of rare occurrence.'

Hodgskin spent time observing the local Maori, whom he found to be friendly and welcoming and even more skilled in the manufacture of fishing gear and flax mats than those in the Bay of Islands. Though the land around Mahurangi was thinly populated, tribes from Thames and other neighbouring areas arrived in season to catch and dry fish and to extract liver oil which they kept in bladders made from the skin of stingrays. Hodgskin bought several gallons of the oil for the ship and reported that it burned 'remarkably well'.

The town of Warkworth is nestled in a gently contoured landscape next to the Mahurangi River. This wonderful spot caught the eye of John Anderson Brown who, in 1853, purchased 153 acres for the town site.

. . . Living in perfect security, treated with respect, and on the most friendly terms with the natives . . .

ABOVE: The river below Warkworth is still an important waterway for both fishing and pleasure boats. Up to the time the metalled road to Auckland was finished, the river was busy with steamboats travelling to and from the city.

LEFT: Recent development in Warkworth has seen the most made of the river and wharf area of the town. This photograph shows that same area in 1945.

TOP: A scene from 1870 showing the landscape after logging. The paling shanty belonged to Peter and Magdalena Bayer of the Upper Waiwera Valley.

ABOVE: Puhoi, with the river right at its doorstep, was an ideal collecting point for logs bound for Auckland sawmills.

BELOW: Much more recently, probably in the early 1960s, Wilf Wech and Alf Rauner take a break while splitting a huge kauri log, presumably for some special occasion.

Men from the *Buffalo* went up the Puhoi and Waiwera rivers and to the forest at the head of the Mahurangi to fell timber. The only Europeans they came upon were a Scot named Browne, and four or five others he employed to saw planks and ready mast timber for the Sydney market.

'Now, here is an instance of six of our countrymen shut out from all intercourse with the civilised world, excepting to the masters of a few small trading vessels who occasionally put in for flax and potatoes, living in perfect security, treated with respect, and on the most friendly terms with the natives,' noted an obviously surprised Hodgskin.

Maori cheerfully dragged six massive spars to the water for the British sailors, and declined muskets in favour of blankets as payment for their work – which may simply have signalled a saturated arms market rather than a pacifist disposition. They were, after all, keen on books, which they rapidly converted into cartridge paper. For the fish and melons that they brought on board, though, they would take in exchange only ship's biscuits.

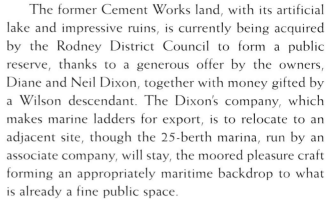

The former Cement Works land, with its artificial lake and impressive ruins, is currently being acquired by the Rodney District Council to form a public reserve, thanks to a generous offer by the owners, Diane and Neil Dixon, together with money gifted by a Wilson descendant. The Dixon's company, which makes marine ladders for export, is to relocate to an adjacent site, though the 25-berth marina, run by an associate company, will stay, the moored pleasure craft forming an appropriately maritime backdrop to what is already a fine public space.

As with other east coast settlements, Warkworth was for years reliant on ships for communication with Auckland, especially in winter, when the roads turned to sludge. Eventually, two rival shipping companies became locked in a price war that split residents into two camps – 'Settlers', who supported the local Coastal Shipping Company, and 'McGregors', who backed the McGregor Steam Ship Company. The clash became very real in 1905 when Alexander McGregor's aptly named *Claymore* ran down the settlers' *Kapanui* in the Waitemata Harbour with the loss of five of its crew.

Warkworth's old wharf at the foot of the town, where farmers once loaded their drays, gigs and traps, lingered on for generations as a reminder of those salty days, its ancient posts and timbered steps decaying amid mangroves and the cushioning mud. Decaying, that is, until locals decided enough was enough and formed the Riverbank Enhancement Group.

In February 1998 a fundraising dinner with a nautical theme and a 320 metre-long table netted $100,000. Dave Parker, one of the organisers, calls the evening 'one of the most rewarding experiences' in his time in Warkworth.

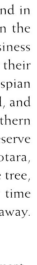

Over coming months the fund almost tripled, and in November that year the new wharf, a showpiece on the town's redeveloping waterfront, opened for business below the new Riverview Plaza. Now, people taking their ease on the timbered structure can watch the Caspian terns and shags that fish the river even this far inland, and contemplate the steep, bush-clad slopes on the northern bank. Here, to the right, the Puhinui Scenic Reserve embraces regenerating forest which includes totara, kanuka, tanekaha and, of course, the town's signature tree, the kowhai. Parker is heartened: 'In the past, every time there was a flood, more of the bank would get taken away. The kowhai were dying. It was a crime.'

LEFT: Riverview Plaza is a recent shopping and café development in Warkworth with views over the new wharf, river and bush-clad hills beyond.

RIGHT: Black shag, a mere stone's throw from Warkworth's main thoroughfare.

While Warkworth's history is intimately tied to the Mahurangi River, it was another, much older, natural resource that helped put the young town on the map: limestone. Formed from a paste of plankton shells gouged from the ocean floor by tectonic plate movements 25 million or more years ago, huge blocks of this muddy limestone finally came to rest around Dairy Flat, Orewa and Warkworth.

SURE TO SET
Wilson's Cement Works

GLASWEGIAN IMMIGRANT NATHANIEL WILSON began playing around with deposits on his land near Warkworth in 1865 as a respite from his shoemaking business. He built kilns to make hydraulic lime and eventually despatched it by the shipload to Auckland where it was in demand for harbour works and construction.

A turning point came in 1883, when Nathaniel was introduced to an engineer's manual on cement-making. Through dogged perseverance this self-taught man and his sons perfected the process and were among the first in the southern hemisphere to manufacture Portland cement.

Following the example of the British, the Wilson & Co Cement Works first packed the cement in barrels, then introduced cotton bags and finally smaller bags of jute. The company nearly came to grief several times, rescuing the situation on one occasion by adding ground pipi shells to the limestone, and on another by changing the type of coke used.

BELOW: 'Riverina' was the home of the founder of the Cement Works, Nathaniel Wilson. It also served as Headquarters for the US Forces stationed in the area from 1943 to 1945.

WILSONS PORTLAND CEMENT WORKS
WARKWORTH. 1407.

ABOVE: The factory workers lived more modestly in these cottages in Pulham Road, nearly all of which have now been moved.

LEFT: The cement works in working condition. It operated from 1872 until 1929 and employed 180 workers.

By 1893 the company had bought all the limestone workings in the area and had put up a new 33-m chimney and 18-m-high kiln. Its 180 workers were by then making 100 tonnes of cement and 100 tonnes of hydraulic lime a week and the company was a driving force in the use of concrete for building in New Zealand. Its 'Star' brand cement was put to work in landmark structures such as the Parnell rail tunnel, Grafton Bridge and the Rangitoto beacon.

But decline was inevitable. Competition had sprung up elsewhere, and limestone deposits near Whangarei Harbour, along with the possibility of electricity generation from the Wairua Falls, prompted a new strategy. The company shifted to Portland, Whangarei in 1928 – later merging with Golden Bay Cement – and the cement works with its kilns, ball mills, laboratories and workshops fell into disuse.

During the Second World War the Home Guard and US forces stationed in the district practised their demolition techniques on the abandoned buildings, transforming them into picturesque ruins. Now the 3-ha site, which contains one of the North Island's most impressive historic industrial remains, is visited by photographers, filmmakers and the curious.

ABOVE: In 1910, when it was built, Auckland's Grafton Bridge was the largest concrete bridge in the world. The cement was made in Warkworth, barged to Auckland, unloaded onto drays and mixed by hand on site.

BELOW: The Stubbs family outside their butchery in 1938. From right to left are: Herbert, Bert, Jim and Joe Stubbs and Jack Phillips. The Stubbs had been in business on this same site from 1922 until 1999.

On the south bank opposite the park stands the venerable Masonic Lodge No 1711, an exotic palm hard by heightening the allure of its neat wooden boards and classical ornaments. Plans to move the Lodge, which dates from 1883, to make way for a civic centre have mercifully stalled. Parker sees a future for the old building as an arts centre, as a part of whatever new complex may emerge. As organiser of the town's Kowhai Festival and a new 'Jazz, Blues and Wine Celebration', he fields any number of enquiries for suitable venues.

The existing town hall, which would strike even a novice as woefully inadequate, has become something of an embarrassment to event promoters. Parker himself sees the need for an outdoor performance area able to accommodate around 450 people.

BELOW LEFT: Cattle have always played a big role in farming around Warkworth. Here, in the 1920s, they await loading at the wharf.

BELOW: The Ramsbottom Stagecoach en route from Warkworth to the Kaipara Flats Railway Station, 1920.

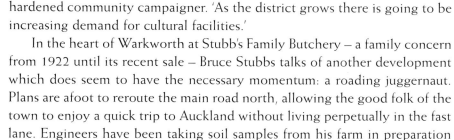

'If the Civic Centre doesn't materialise, a new group of locals will swing into action to get things going,' says Parker, sounding every bit the hardened community campaigner. 'As the district grows there is going to be increasing demand for cultural facilities.'

In the heart of Warkworth at Stubb's Family Butchery – a family concern from 1922 until its recent sale – Bruce Stubbs talks of another development which does seem to have the necessary momentum: a roading juggernaut. Plans are afoot to reroute the main road north, allowing the good folk of the town to enjoy a quick trip to Auckland without living perpetually in the fast lane. Engineers have been taking soil samples from his farm in preparation for the diversion. It seems that when not actively seeking to lure roads in their direction, the townships of Rodney are busy getting some distance from them. It is a continual dance with the roadmakers.

The photographer Tudor Collins, whose house and studio once stood not far from the Stubbs establishment, is best-known for having documented the breaking-in of the northern North Island, from the logging of kauri and gumdigging to the tenanting of the land with animals. Many of his glass plates are now in the Warkworth and District Museum, along with his Graflex camera and his massive Eastman Kodak projection printer.

Collins was in large measure responsible for preserving Parry Kauri Park, in which the well-stocked museum stands; a photograph of his appeared in the *Weekly News* drawing attention to the plight of several massive kauri destined to be felled for boat-building. The photograph resulted in a flood of donations from across New Zealand that helped save the trees, one of

them estimated to be 800 years old, and the nearest large kauri to Auckland city. The 2-ha park now has impressive boardwalks threading through its stands of regenerating kauri and kahikatea.

A chronicler of change, Collins was more aware than most people of where the district was heading, but even he may have raised an eyebrow if he could have seen ahead to the industrial parks a few kilometres away from his beloved trees.

Here, on the other side of State Highway One at Glenmore Drive and Hudson Road, are businesses ranging from a fitness centre and aluminium joinery manufacturers to automotive services and electrical contractors. The New Zealand icon 'Buzzy Bee' is there, as is Times Colour Print, New Zealand's third biggest printer and one of Warkworth's major employers – the company also owns the *Rodney Times* newspaper.

ABOVE LEFT: The Warkworth Rodeo has been going every year since 1960 and intends to be the first in the world to strut its stuff in the new millennium.

LEFT: Extensive pine forests flank the hills to the south of Woodcocks Road in the very heart of Rodney District. This, the largest of them, is owned by Rodney Forests and occupies more than 200 ha.

One of the more unusual companies at Glenmore Drive is The Forge, an iron foundry run by a German community, Homeward Bound, which makes what it calls 'one-off iron artworks'. Most of these hand-beaten originals, in the form of ornately sculpted gates and furniture, are exported to places such as Brunei, Malaysia and Singapore. In 1993 the 'Paradise Gate', by ironmaster Stefan Steinmetz and his wife Elizabeth, who applies finishing patinas, won the International Masterpiece Award, one of seven trophies competed for in 80 countries. A riot of parrots and grapes, the gate is typical of their pieces which can take six months or more to complete. Just up the road is the Rodney Health Enterprise Trust. Started by Wendy Hawkings, the trust took the unusual step of buying a motel for conversion to residential units, on-selling them to people not yet ready for rest homes. 'There is a gap in the Warkworth market for people whose homes have got too much for them,' says office administrator Wendy Waldron. As well as being on-call to residents, the trust also offers home care for hospital patients and the elderly from Wenderholm to Mangawhai and coast to coast. The motel courtyard, leading to a sauna, spa and decked pool, is finished with wrought iron railings and a cheerful rooster on a wrought iron frame – reminders of the previous owners, Stefan and Elizabeth, who bought the business on their arrival in New Zealand and later sold it to the trust in order to buy a farm in Wellsford for their community.

Opposite the instantly recognisable satellite station just south of Warkworth, is another entrepreneurial venture, the Honey Centre, which boasts the biggest live bee display in the country – a wall of 50,000 workers behind glass. 'Big staff, isn't it,' quips owner Kerry Fountain. 'The trouble is, they only live six weeks.'

Fountain started fooling with bees at the age of seven when a swarm landed in his Pukekohe backyard. 'My parents hated me doing bees and didn't think I'd make a living,' says the man who now sells all the honey he can get – 60 tonnes last year, including manuka, rewarewa, tawari, clover and dark bush honey.

The 17-ha property was in kiwifruit when Kerry and his wife Wilma bought it, but the vines went, to be replaced by the Honey Centre, an adjoining café and, just up the hill, Greg's Sheep-N-Show.

Greg Clark, the driving force behind the original Sheep World, set up the new venture to keep doing what he does best – run sheep and dog shows. Nationwide, only two venues outside Warkworth offer similar shows, Rotorua's Agridome and Rainbow Springs.

While Romney and Drysdale and black-faced Suffolk practise being sheep in a nearby paddock, Clark chews over the benefits of the present location. The proximity of the satellite station and the honey centre mean the three things can be packaged together. School groups can call in on their way to either of the two camps at Snells Beach. And then there is the new motorway to Puhoi.

'You have to be in this for the long haul,' says Clark. 'And a lot of our regulars have baches or boats up here. They treat Rodney as their playground.'

The first wrought iron piece Stefan and Elizabeth Steinmetz made is on a property up the back of Greg's Sheep-N-Show. A double gate with sheep. It seems a perfect entrance for a playground.

Custom-made for Rodney.

TOP: Stefan Steinmetz at work at The Forge, known for its internationally recognised masterpieces in iron.

ABOVE: Sheepworld, along with Sheep-N-Show, attract hundreds of visitors each week during the summer months.

BELOW: Visitors to the Honey Centre just south of Warkworth viewing the biggest live bee display in the country.

It has been called New Zealand's most beautiful tree. Its medicinal qualities were well-known to Maori and its bell-like flower has become the national flower of New Zealand. It is the kowhai, and in spring its golden blooms adorn Rodney, where the yearly spectacle of their unfolding has become a useful pretext for holding a festival.

FLOWER POWER
Kowhai Festival

THE WARKWORTH AND DISTRICTS ANNUAL KOWHAI FESTIVAL, to give it its full dress title, is an extravaganza of wine, food, markets and entertainment which sprawls over a week or more and culminates in a street parade. Festival Day, the highlight of the festival, attracts 25,000 or more people from throughout Rodney and beyond and pumps an estimated $1.2 million into its economy.

Dave Parker, who helped set the whole thing in motion back in 1970 with a float parade, and who has laboured on it most of its 29 years, says Warkworth is one of the few communities that has managed to retain a sense of continuity and community involvement.

'Certainly it is the only annual festival that has been going nearly 30 years without missing a beat, thanks largely to the driving force of a few people determined to succeed.'

Thanks also to the blooms that never fail.

ABOVE: The Band of the Royal NZ Artillery are one of many to march in the big parade. Others include the Kumeu and Warkworth Brass Bands and the 'kiwis' (below left), of the Guggenmusik Auckland Band.

PLAYGROUND FOR THE PEOPLE

MAHURANGI HARBOUR
TO GOAT ISLAND

The height of summer at Goat Island where thousands come to see, and even feed, the fish.

BELOW: This majestic pohutukawa overlooks the entrance to Mahurangi Harbour, as it's done for 100 years.

*M*ahurangi Heads on a fine summer's morning, with the brilliant bloom of pohutukawa contrasting with the blue water of the harbour, and with the vista of winding rivers and bluff headlands in the distance, is as near to paradise as poor mortals can expect to get in this life.

NEW ZEALAND HERALD, 1923

Mansion House on Kawau Island is one of the most beautiful colonial houses north of Auckland. Both it and the grounds have been lovingly restored and are maintained by the Department of Conservation.

A little way north of Warkworth, State Highway One enters Dome Valley. From the Dome Tearooms carpark on the crest of the hill a walkway leads to a lookout with vistas of Mahurangi Peninsula and the Hauraki Gulf. People with an adventurous disposition can continue up a steeper track to the craggy 336-m Dome summit which offers views of plantation forest and the outer Hauraki Gulf.

Maori lore identifies the Dome as a resting place for the Tainui ancestor Reipae who, with her sister Reitu, flew to Whangarei Harbour on the back of a bird. Travellers in Rodney these days may have adopted more mundane transport, but often their goal is similar: to add spice to lives hemmed by routine.

To do this, many people turn right at Warkworth and take one of two roads. The first leads to Sandspit and the Mahurangi Peninsula; the second to Matakana and the small coastal settlements beyond.

Sandspit, named for a finger of sand at the mouth of the Matakana River, is the gateway to historic Kawau Island, the former island bolthole of George Grey, one of New Zealand's towering nineteenth century figures. Visitors ferried from Sandspit wharf can savour the immaculately restored mansion and its tranquil tree-studded grounds and saunter along one of the island's gentle walking tracks. En route to Mansion House Bay, or to Bon Accord Harbour, if they are tagging along on the mail run, ferry passengers can take in the extravagant new houses built on the northern bluffs of the Mahurangi Peninsula.

Scotts Landing reverberated to the echo of shipbuilders' hammers 150 years ago; today, the only sounds are the chatter of birdsong and the gentle lapping of the tide.

At Snells Beach and Algies Bay old baches stand alongside more recent houses above good swimming beaches, a reminder of the days when this part of Rodney was even more of a secluded getaway than it is now. Beyond Mullet Point and the attractive camping ground of Martins Bay, where in 1943 American marines piled ashore as a warmup to landings in the Solomons, a ridge road leads through farmland to Mahurangi Heads.

Not far off, at the end of a thin needle of land probing Mahurangi Harbour is Scotts Landing. Here, in the mid-1850s, Thomas Scott and his two sons built a home and got a shipyard going. Shipbuilding was a common activity on this coast until the early 1900s – three of the region's most active yards were in nearby Te Kapa Inlet – and as if to underscore

the industry's importance, the Scotts put up a hotel, the 'Richmond Arms', to cater for shipyard and timber workers as well as seabound travellers.

In 1873 the hotel burned down, as hotels tended to do in those days – think of Silverdale's Wade Hotel, or the hotel at Waiwera – and it was replaced four years later by a boarding establishment known today as Scott House. In 1971, after serving time as a private residence, the two-storeyed wooden building was bought and restored by the Auckland Regional Authority. The oldest coastal boarding house in Rodney, it is now available for short-term hire from the ARA's successor, the Auckland Regional Council, along with several cottages.

. . . often their goal is similar: to add spice to lives hemmed by routine

TOP: Five species of wallaby were liberated on Kawau Island in the latter part of the nineteenth century; at least three still thrive, and one of them – the parma wallaby – is being exported to its native Australia where it is now rare.

ABOVE LEFT: The Darroch shipyard at Whangateau was part of the flourishing shipbuilding industry along this part of the coast at the end of the nineteenth century. In this 1902 photograph the *Eunice* appears to be undergoing repairs while at left the skeleton of a new vessel is being assembled.

LEFT: A copse of mighty kauri greet walkers at the end of the roller-coaster Dome Valley Walkway.

BELOW: Anthony Morris settled in the Matakana Valley in 1977 and established the commercial pottery of Morris and James. A small sample of their colourful hand-thrown pots can be seen right.

TOP: Visitors are welcome to drop by the factory and café and, for those with a geological bent, a guide can explain how the clay used to make the pots was transformed from volcanic ash that showered the area 20 million years ago.

ABOVE: Remains of an old scow, identified as the *Lake St Clair*, were discovered in the mud of the estuary nearby. This vessel was one of several scows built in the Mahurangi Harbour about 1876 and used as a tow-barge around the turn of the century before coming to grief in the early 1930s.

Breathtaking vistas of the Hauraki Gulf are one of the attractions along this coast, as is identifying the numerous islands. This is beach-fringed Saddle Island (Te Haupu) between the Mahurangi Heads and Motuora Island.

Which is a good thing, because there is a bit to do out on this limb of the Mahurangi: nothing that would get signposted, necessarily, but then that characterises the charm of this corner of the district. Visitors can swim, fish, watch gannets and terns show how fishing is really done, poke about Casnell Island's Maunganui Pa at low tide and, if they are more than a little favoured, hitch a ride out to Motuora Island on the Motuora Restoration Society's new inflatable, bought thanks to a generous private donation.

The little-known Motuora Island, farmed until World War Two, became a recreational reserve in 1966. It was later found to be predator-free and in 1995 the Restoration Society was formed to reforest the 80-ha island on behalf of DoC, with the goal of transforming it into a wildlife sanctuary on the model of nearby Tiritiri Matangi Island. Volunteers have so far established some 45,000 plants and the island is shortly to be used as a kiwi crèche. In the long term it is hoped to introduce native birds as well as ten endangered lizard species, tuatara, giant weta, giant centipedes and other insects.

Turning from the Mahurangi Peninsula, the second of the two roads climbing east out of Warkworth leads to Matakana, itself a gateway of sorts to economic activities that in more straight-jacketed days would have been labelled 'alternative' – things like hydroponics and tile workshops, palm gardens, ostrich farms and reptile parks, marine educationalists and flash cafés in old sawmills.

Morris and James, a stone's throw beyond Matakana, is as good a place as any to get acquainted with the region's diversity. One of the country's more successful potteries, it specialises in decorative tiles and handthrown pots, many of them colourfully glazed.

Anthony Morris started the business in 1977 when he settled in the Matakana Valley and began working clay deposits on his property. In a sense, he was picking up where the pioneers had left off. In 1864 George Manners, a local farmer, had begun a small brickworks on the site and Morris has found evidence of his clay excavations and clamp kilns and possibly the location of his horse-operated processing machinery.

Another unusual find made in the estuary mud nearby was the skeletal remains of an old sailing vessel, later identified as the *Lake St Clair* (1876), one of the first scows to be built in New Zealand.

In the distant past Toi te Huatahi named the island Te Kawau tu maro,
'the shag that stands sentinel'. But Kawau might equally have been called
Motomuru for the small spotted basking shark that was once plentiful in its
sheltered waters. It was caught in huge quantities by Maori and local Pakeha,
and hundreds at a time could be seen drying on flax lines at Sandspit.

A Jewel in the Crown
Kawau Island

Day trippers arriving at
Mansion House Bay.

THE LOCAL KAWERAU PEOPLE and southern Hauraki Gulf tribes had fought over the prized fishing grounds since the 1720s, but when the missionary Samuel Marsden set foot on Kawau in 1820, he found the island's pa abandoned.

James Cook and the French explorer D'Urville had both mistaken the island for part of the mainland, but later settlers were not so easily fooled about its potential. Bought in 1840 for sheepfarming, it was soon found to have big deposits of manganese and copper. Cornish miners arrived in 1846 to work the green veins and help found what became the country's first export industry, with 1200 tonnes of copper shipped in that first year alone. Soon after, Welsh smelterers from Swansea took up residence, building a sizeable smelting works, now reduced to ruin, in Bon Accord Harbour. Other reminders of those early years include a restored pumphouse chimney, now once again a prominent landmark on the southern coast.

George Grey, soldier, statesman, philanthropist, explorer and governor of three nations, bought Kawau in 1862 as a refuge from the slings and arrows of public life. He rebuilt the mine manager's cottage, turning it into the imposing residence now known as Mansion House. Grey sunk his fortune into Kawau, stocking his house with rare books and art, and the lawns with exotic plants such as Chilean wine palms, a holm oak, Indian deodars and an African coral tree. A bizarre animal menagerie crowded the parklike grounds, including emu, elk, wapiti, zebras and monkeys. Whenever he could, Grey retreated to his island jewel, which he delighted in showing off to distinguished visitors and often opened to the public.

Ill health forced Grey to sell in 1888, and later owners tried to make a living by subdividing the island and by running Grey's home as a guest house. During the 1920s and 1930s Kawau became a magnet for weekend excursions from Auckland, and to this day it is one of the most popular Hauraki Gulf destinations for boaties. Daytrippers also make use of regular ferry services from Sandspit and from Auckland 60 km to the south.

Though most of Grey's animals have gone, the kookaburra still thrive and the hardy possums and wallabies continue to take their toll on the island's forest remnants. In 1979, however, the Hauraki Gulf Maritime Park Board chalked up a victory over some of Kawau's human tenants when, having ripped out years of unsightly alterations, it reopened the painstakingly restored Mansion House as a National Trust property. With 60 private jetties and a permanent population of around 80, Kawau remains, as it was in George Grey's day, a roadless refuge for those seeking solitude.

TOP: Sir George Edward Grey, who made Kawau his home and in so doing created one of the most visited islands of the Hauraki Gulf.

MIDDLE: Bon Accord Harbour and the coastline of Kawau are a mecca for Auckland boaties. Night races are held from Auckland to Kawau at Easter.

RIGHT: The chimney of the old coppermine is one of New Zealand's earliest industrial ruins. The mine had already closed when Governor Grey bought the island in 1862.

RIGHT: The lime-washed adobe home of Joe Polaischer and Trish Allen is a prime example of their philosophy of sustainability. Even the sod-roof provides a perfect habitat for herbs and succulents. Rainbow Valley Farm north of Matakana is permaculture farming in action.

Visitors with an interest in geology or in making things in the backyard can take a tour of the Morris and James backyard – a place called the clay paddock. Here a guide will explain how 20 million years ago three volcanoes of the North Island's west coast showered the area with ash. Back then the paddock and surrounding land formed the bed of a shallow sea and the ash was gradually transformed into sandstone. In that complicated way geology has of going about things, plate tectonics pushed the sea floor up to fashion hills and through weathering some of the sandstone's minerals were transformed into clay. The clay was then washed into the river where it collected and compacted.

Now, once every couple of years, workers drive a backhoe into the paddock and carve out 1000 tonnes or so of clay from the high terraces, sun-dry it, crush it, sieve it, add a prefired grit called 'grog' and set about making more pots and tiles.

The land around Matakana has always been good for crops as well as crockery. In the mid-years of last century Alexander Campbell, a young migrant who arrived aboard the *Tornado*, wrote to family back in Scotland describing his experiences and the doings of a fellow passenger named Croker.

'We were very amused at Mrs Kilso and you thinking that if we had only plenty of potatoes we might get on, but the bush affords a more varied supply – perhaps you are not aware that in the colony folks live pretty well,' wrote Campbell teasingly.

'It's all part of our philosophy to turn what are usually thought of as problem species into an advantage'

Fruit trees had been planted, he added, and 'in two seasons Mr Croker will have as many peaches, apples, figs, plums, apricots, melons, etc, as he is able to use. Adjoining the garden is a field of three acres covered with a sward of grass which will be ready in a month for putting a cow or two on'.

Timber and fruit underpinned settler livelihoods for many years, but early this century fly-borne fire blight destroyed the fruit industry. With no pesticides available to check the disease, growers ripped out their trees and turned to dairying.

These days, talk of pesticides would get a cold hearing from Joe Polaischer, one of Matakana's new generation of agriculturists. Joe and his partner Trish Allen are exponents of permaculture, the holistic approach to living which takes as its guiding principle environmentally responsible farming or sustainability. It might more poetically be described as 'treading lightly on the earth'.

Their showcase property, Rainbow Valley Farm, is a 21-ha slice of land embraced by 160 m-high bush-clad hills and reached by a winding shingle road north of Matakana. A sod-roofed house lime-washed adobe bricks, immediately announces their philosophy. Dug into a hill and capped with a living roof of herbs and succulents, it almost dissolves into the landscape.

The beginnings of the permaculture project, though, were not auspicious. When the couple bought the farm it was in a rundown state and they lived in a house truck, surrounded by two of nature's 'nightmares' – gorse and kikuyu grass.

ABOVE: Exotic species as well as natives thrive in the luxuriant gardens of Rainbow Valley Farm.

LEFT: Joe Polaischer made a name for himself in the district with a feature in a local paper headed 'Ten Good Points About Gorse.'

'It's all part of our philosophy to turn what are usually thought of as problem species into an advantage,' says Joe, who once wrote a feature for the community paper headed 'Ten Good Points About Gorse'. 'That got our local farmers going,' he says wryly. For the record, gorse is an excellent nitrogen fixer and protects nesting birds such as waxeyes and fantails from cats and possums, and kikuyu is a good mulch. Chainsawing, seeding ground cover, mowing and shading with trees will get rid of gorse when the time comes, he says.

Joe and Trish have planted more than 10,000 timber trees on their property, and the couple milk cows and harvest fruit and nuts from a large orchard. But it is hard to single out a dominant activity. Pilgrim and weeder geese keep orchard grass down, bantams, guinea fowl and kunekune pigs control pests, Tamworth pigs, Rhode Island reds and Muscovy ducks provide meat. Then there are the bees, the eels, the freshwater mussels and the edible pond plants.

Which is how it should be. Rainbow Valley Farm is not about economies of scale or mono-cropping but about working with nature. 'If we attack nature we attack ourselves and ultimately destroy our environment,' Joe once wrote in a primer on sustainable living. He is not about to soften his views.

If environmental responsibility is the theme at Rainbow Valley Farm, at Heron's Flight Vineyard near the Matakana River the watchword is conviviality. There, on north-facing slopes Pennsylvania-born David Hoskins and his partner Mary Evans make Italian-style reds.

David came to Matakana in the mid-1980s when a vineyard at Tomarata Lake in Wellsford was up for sale. Nothing came of that, but David heard of another vineyard – The Antipodean – which was about to go into production in Matakana. He liked the area and thought the ground suited viticulture, so bought the seven hectares to start Heron's Flight – named for a family of herons living in pines down by the inlet.

The early wines enjoyed critical success and a respectable number of awards, and since 1994 they have experimented with Italian grape varieties – Sangiovese and Montepulciano. But David and Mary soon withdrew from retail outlets to concentrate on the sympathetic presentation of their wines at the vineyard. That means informally and in the context of food such as smoked salmon platters and panini breads.

David tends to wax philosophical about wine and its cultural importance. 'Wine is never an end in itself for us,' he says. 'It is always the means to another end – conviviality.' The first plantings at Heron's Flight were assisted by a libation of wine and prefaced by a reading from Plato's *Symposium* on the theme of love, 'all done in the context of consuming large quantities of wine'.

It is a sociability the owners of Heron's Flight are keen to spread around. They hold regular group tastings and in early 1999 hosted a ten-day Matakana celebration that included performances by Gary McCormick, Hammond Gamble and blues guitarist Alan Young, a barrel race in Kawau Bay and a scarecrow-making workshop. The scarecrows were auctioned off and all proceeds given to an arts group attempting to restore Warkworth's Masonic Lodge. A highlight of the week was an evening of wine under the stars at Scotts Landing, featuring industry notables and meals prepared by invited chefs.

Matakana will never attract the big wine companies, says David, because the clay soils necessitate planting on slopes and can't be heavily mechanised. 'But if you are careful with what you plant you can still make good wine.' He takes a piece of paper and sketches a rough triangle from Warkworth out towards Matakana and across in the direction of Sandspit. He then numbers the vineyards, getting up to ten before he stops with a smile. 'Others are coming on stream and there is a queue of people looking for land to start up.'

It would be wrong, however, to linger over wine – alluring though it is – at the expense of other fruits of the land. Matakana is home to crops such as hydroponic lettuces and capsicum, as well as hydroponic roses and hothouse tomatoes for export.

Sangiovese, Montepulciano, *La Dolca Vita*. Heron's Flight (top) and Brick Bay, two of the new breed of vineyards in the Warkworth area, look out over Kawau Bay and manage quite comfortably to give the impression that all is well with the world.

INSET: Snapper, here chilled and ready for export, are just one of the many fish species landed at Leigh Harbour.

On the east coast, out towards Cape Rodney, is a small picturesque cove known to early Maori as Omaha, which roughly translates as 'the place of plenty'.

Home these days to a sizeable fishing fleet as well as to numerous pleasure craft, Leigh Harbour, as it is now called, is a safe deep-water anchorage protected from all but the strongest sou'easters.

INSET: Snapper, here chilled and ready for export, are just one of the many fish species landed at Leigh Harbour.

DAVY JONES' LARDER
Leigh Harbour

Snapper, tuna and live lobsters along with an array of other fish species are landed at the wooden wharf for processing at Leigh Fisheries up the road. The company, which employs one in five of the fishing village's population, specialises in airfreighting chilled seafood to markets in Asia, Europe and the United States.

In the belly of the cove stands the attractive Te Kiri Marae, maintained by local Ngati Wai, whose ancestral ground this is. Pioneering missionaries favoured the cove as a stopover during their coastal travels and in the 1860s and 1870s sailing vessels built in McQuarrie and McInnes' shipyard on the sandy flat reinforced the tie with the sea.

On a narrow stretch of land jutting into the Whangateau Harbour, fenced with towering bamboo shelterbelts and culminating in the tranquil beauty of Point Wells, 'the Garden Village', is something more unexpected – the 4-ha Longwood Palm Garden. At the end of a long palm-lined avenue, under 1000 square metres of shadecloth as well as in the open, are any number of palms, orchids and fuchsias. In season, many of these can be surveyed from a seat in the garden's café, also under shadecloth.

Tim Rowsell, who started Longwood in 1982, specialises in kentias and other collectable palms which he ships as far as the South Island – yes, some species will grow beyond Cook Strait. Prices range from $30 for a small specimen of the popular queen palm up to $3,000.

Across the harbour from Longwood is Ti Point, home of Ti Point Reptile Park. There, proprietor Ivan Borich, who has kept house for unorthodox creatures for the best part of 25 years, is likely to be found cleaning out turtle cages or tossing food to a 'gator.

He began with a range of beasts, including zebras, bison and all sorts of other mammals, and a few remain. Ambling down the pleasant bush-walk the visitor is likely to be startled by the conversation of a parrot or the antics of a pair of capuchin monkeys. But two years ago Ivan decided to specialise in breeding and displaying reptiles. 'The monkeys will go when I find them a good home,' says Ivan stoically.

He is at work now on a nocturnal house for tuatara and claims to have a greater range of New Zealand reptile species than any of the country's major zoos, including the endangered robust skink and the larger Three Kings Islands skink, which is considered to be at risk. Then there are the Reeves turtle, a native of China, the box tortoise, Australian shingleback skinks, water dragons and many more.

It is almost worth negotiating Ivan's drive for the bush-walk and the ridge view of Omaha Bay which, on a clear day, is a dazzling blue. Of course, the indented shoreline affords this chunk of Rodney an uncommon number of sea vistas. There are a dozen or more beaches within half an hour's drive of Warkworth, and one of the most arresting is Omaha's four-kilometre band of shelving white sand. American marines stormed ashore here to limber up for Iwo Jima and other Pacific landings during the war, but the beach, with its modern surf club and curling breakers has forgotten all that.

Omaha Peninsula is one of the region's few breeding sites for the endangered New Zealand dotterel – another being Whakanewha Regional

ABOVE: Ivan Borich of the Ti Point Reptile Park with an assortment of exotic creatures.

OPPOSITE: Unspoilt beaches skirt the spectacular coastline of Tawharanui Regional Park.

BELOW: Omaha's sandy spit is home to the endangered New Zealand dotterel; feet should be placed with care.

Park on Waiheke. In 1999, for the first time in seven years, two chicks survived to fledge at Omaha, thanks to a public education programme, the appointment of wardens and the building of a vehicle barrier. Their future, however, is still not assured.

The dotterels can also be seen in the region's biggest coastal farm park, Tawharanui, out towards Takatu Point. The park incorporates a Marine Protected Area, the first of its kind, and offers walks through regenerating kauri and tanekaha, and alongside a raupo wetland. Birds going about their business here include spotless crake, bittern, reef heron and paradise shelduck.

The Auckland Regional Council recently
branded its parks 'Natural Masterpieces'
and in choice open air spots put up big baroque
frames to highlight the views. It is not surprising,
given the district's attractive and varied coasts,
that five of the most popular parks are in Rodney.

OH I DO LIKE TO BE BESIDE THE SEA
ARC Parks

Tawharanui Regional Park, a farm park of soft contours,
rugged coast, unspoilt beaches and glorious views over the Gulf.

SHAKESPEAR AND TAWHARANUI are coastal farm parks offering camping and safe swimming as well as fine gulf vistas. Shakespear's marshy lowlands, on Whangaparaoa Peninsula, are home to one of the country's largest populations of pukeko, while the park's rolling hills are grazed by Coopworth sheep and Hereford cattle.

The pastures at Tawharanui, which caps the Tawharanui Peninsula near Warkworth, drop to gnarled reefs, shingle-strewn bays and sandy beaches. Here, the country's first Marine Protected Area embraces marine life on the reefs and northern coast while an ecology trail winds through wetland, broadleaf forest and regenerating bush. Sizeable Jones Bay lagoon owes its existence to a century of shingle extraction.

LEFT: Mahurangi Regional Park is divided into West and East (separated by the entrance to Mahurangi Harbour). The area has a rich history of Maori occupation, evidenced by the many archaeological sites.

BELOW: These gentle dunelands, a vulnerable barrier between black sand and pine forest, belie the wild, west-coast nature of Muriwai Regional Park. The park offers something different to more than a million visitors a year.

BOTTOM: Shakespear Regional Park established in 1967 as a farm park, sits at the tip of Whangaparaoa Peninsula, with spectacular views to Auckland City and the outlying islands of the Gulf.

Picture-perfect Wenderholm, a day-tripper's haven at the mouth of the Puhoi River, became Auckland's first regional park in 1965. On the estuary a nineteenth century pohutukawa plantation – New Zealand's largest – shades picnickers, while the fruit of the park's lush coastal forest are a magnet for kereru, the native pigeon.

To the north lies Mahurangi, a park safeguarding three peninsulas at the entrance to the Mahurangi Harbour. The quiet coastal landscape is popular with boaties and hosts the Mahurangi Regatta in January. It is also rich in history, with fortified pa sites and building remains.

On the opposite coast, Muriwai's black sands fringe the Tasman surf for 48 km, terminating in one of the country's best-known gannet sanctuaries. Muriwai Regional Park offers a total contrast to other parks, with a million or more visitors a year enjoying the chance to swim, surf, fish and take in the natural beauty.

LEFT: Wenderholm is renowned for its pohutukawa-lined beach and diverse bird life which draw thousands of picnickers each year. It is also the home of the beautifully restored Couldrey House.

Omaha is one of the most spectacular beaches in the area, with a 4-km band of white sand looking out across the sparkling blue waters of the Hauraki Gulf to Little Barrier Island.

A little further north, towards Leigh, is Matheson Bay, named for one of the Nova Scotian families who settled the area in the late 1850s. Its original Maori name, Kohuroa, is a reference to the sea mist that sometimes curtains the bay. Matheson Bay is the best place in Rodney to see fossils, including those of giant oysters, sea egg spines and corals, all of which are visible in rocks north and south of the beach.

Here too, is the surviving house built by Angus Matheson who, with a business partner, started a shipyard, established farms and put up homes in the bay. Since then the bay has at times been called home by people like television personalities Hudson and Hall, Rod Dixon, who still organises a yearly fun run at Leigh and, more recently, by Times Media owner Tony Cook. Squadron Leader Trent, VC, gained respect in the Bay some years ago when he had a cliff-top home built. 'He was warned he would get the wind,' says one local. 'But it just curled over the top. I guess he knew his aerodynamics.'

In season the beach is a magnet for picnickers, including Pacific Islanders who add colour with spread tapa cloths. Indeed, over summer so many people come to places like Matheson Bay and to the magnificent nearby Goat Island Marine Reserve that some peace-loving locals feel hard done by.

Not so the Sawmill Café in Leigh, a family business which caters for divers and city folk with a craving for something different. The café owed a lot to serendipity according to principal chef, Annabelle Randle, whose father Grattan Guinness heads the operation. Leigh was Annabelle's child-hood turf and having helped run well-known Auckland restaurant Oblio's for three years as a family operation, she was keen to get back to the coast.

TOP AND ABOVE: The moods of Matheson Bay, near Leigh, can change according to the winds, but when an easterly raises the spume holidaymakers can simply duck into the tranquil backwaters of Whangateau Harbour. The contrast couldn't be greater.

Nothing captures quintessential New Zealand better than the sight of a modest weathered bach tucked into some pristine tree-fringed bay. Rodney has no shortage of either beaches or baches, but they are both at their sundrenched best just east of Warkworth.

BEACHES AND BACHES
Warkworth

FROM THE CLIFF EDGE HOLIDAY HOMES of Algies Bay to the improvised homes of Whangateau and the orderly abodes of Point Wells, Matakana is a haven for exhausted city folk and retirees alike. Its sea margins seem to collect old homes the way some mantelpieces collect curios.

And yet, even here, baches of the new order are making inroads. Large, architect-designed buildings that exude wealth are staking claims on prime sites, altering the scale and feel of places that once knew solitude and a priceless empty beauty. Locked up for the mostpart, though not abandoned, they patiently face seaward awaiting the seasonal visit of their preoccupied owners.

The quintessential Kiwi holiday is a bach by the beach. East of Warkworth baches of every shape, size and colour, old and new, grand and modest, adorn the coastline.

Sometimes the sea strikes back, as when in July 1978 a high tide whipped up by a strong easterly stormed ashore at Omaha turning a protective pine seawall to matchwood and clawing at house foundations.

The damage there has since been repaired and Omaha again looks like the upmarket ocean development it once was. But elsewhere the old character-filled baches live on, a reminder of another, less hurried era.

'We'd been coming up here to dive for ten years, watching divers get changed in front of the general store and eat pies and ice cream,' says Annabelle's husband Phil. 'That's what convinced us this would be viable.'

When a local sawmill was put on the market the idea grew of setting up a dive lodge. The mill, which had a native timber quota, was bought along with 3.5 ha of land. A dive centre was opened nearby to fill tanks, hire out gear and fix anything that got broken. Then the family set about landscaping the grounds and restoring the turn-of-the-century mill which had been moved up from the Leigh wharf in the 1930s, working it for six months to cut timber for the renovations. The restaurant itself is in what was once called 'the skids' and diners share the mezzanine with an impressive saw.

The menu takes advantage of the proliferation of nearby herb growers, poultry farmers and hydroponics gardeners as well as local seafood exporter Leigh Fisheries, to conjure up innovative resort-style dishes such as fresh roasted tomato soup with crostini, blue cod grilled with fennel and caviar oil, and mussel and calamari stir fry. Being a sawmill the newly installed pizza oven is, naturally, woodfired.

'We are their only local customer, so they flick us off all the strange stuff: moonfish, baramundi, tuna,' says Phil. 'When the importers from Japan come over on business they even bring their own seafood from the fisheries to have it cooked here.'

And Leigh Fisheries is all about getting fish – whole fish, not fillets – on overseas shelves. The company works with the crews of 70 longline fishing boats, 30 of them local, the rest from as far afield as Whangaroa Harbour and Wanganui and air-exports 3000 tonnes of snapper and other inshore species a year as well as 100 tonnes of live lobsters. Within 36 hours of being pulled from the water the catch is in the hands of customers in markets from Japan, Korea and Taiwan, to Europe and the United States.

The 50-year-old company – known in Japan as Lee Fisheries – prides itself on having the best fishing fleet in the country. 'We are unique,' says general manager Greg Bishop. 'The last bastion of independence in the fishing industry.'

'Twenty years ago we needed the sea.
Now, the sea needs us.
All our profits go toward saving it.'

ABOVE: One of the 30 local boats that make up part of the fishing fleet of Leigh Fisheries. This successful seafood exporter operates out of Leigh's picturesque harbour in the shelter of Cape Rodney.

LEFT: Pleasure boats at anchor in the shelter of Leigh Harbour.

For all its market savvy, Leigh Fisheries comes across as being community oriented. 'We could easily pick this company up and put it in Auckland next to the airport,' says Greg. He shrugs. With one in five of Leigh's population employed by the fishery it is something of a company village. Then there is the Leigh pre-school and primary. 'I always make sure I have some money for them.'

On the hills overlooking Goat Island is someone whose charity is directed toward the sea itself. More than 20 years ago dive enthusiast Floor Anthoni and his wife Maria bought 10 ha here within a snorkel swing of the marine reserve. Plans for retirement faded for the Dutch couple in 1990 when they created Seafriends, an organisation aimed at championing marine environmentalism. Seafriends is housed in a converted shearing shed, with dive gear for hire stored in rooms at ground level and a café above – walled with a marine library – that converts into a classroom for school groups. Out back is a room of linked seawater aquariums containing 150 species in different habitats – an experiment in running a self-contained world.

'I was warned by scientists that it couldn't be done so, being a Dutchman, I needed to do it,' he says with a laugh. But at bottom there is a seriousness to everything Floor does. New Zealand's seas are deteriorating badly, he says. Not from exploitation these days so much as from land pollution and erosion.

'Twenty years ago we needed the sea. Now, the sea needs us,' he says. 'All our profits go toward saving it.'

So it goes. Whether it is wine or reptiles, sea life or the clay beneath their feet, people in these parts seem uncommonly gifted at finding passion in life. And those from elsewhere who make the effort, find an uncommonly good playground.

FAR LEFT: The Sawmill Café at Leigh is a popular stop for visitors to nearby Goat Island marine reserve (above). The turn-of-the-century-mill provides the atmosphere and Phil Randle (shown) and wife Annabelle provide sumptuous local foods.

A FISH BOWL
OFF THE COAST

Goat Island Marine Reserve

**Twenty years ago it was little more than a
wilderness of kina, a virtually lifeless underwater
desert. Now the sea around Goat Island
(Motu Hawere) is thick with corals, seaweed,
rays, octopus and, above all, fish.**

Not far from shore a bewildering array of fish, including snapper, kahawai, gurnard, blue maomao, leatherjackets, red moki and kelpfish, can be seen going about their business among the richly carpeted rocks.

The change came about as the result of a simple plea to stop commercial and recreational fishing along this stretch of coast and give battered nature a chance to restock. The radical idea, put forward by University of Auckland's John Morton and Val Chapman, was quickly taken up in 1965 by Bill Ballantine, resident biologist at the university's newly opened Leigh marine laboratory which overlooked the island.

But creating what was in effect the country's first underwater national park by reversing the overfishing begun by spearfishers and others in the 1950s turned out to be no easy matter. Commercial fishers talked gloomily of the damage to their livelihood and the local paper announced that such legislation would cause a recreational desert – that there would no longer be anything to do at Goat Island bay.

After years of argument the sanctuary, with the unwieldy official name of the Cape Rodney to Okakari Point Marine Reserve, opened in May 1977. Two decades later the early objections have proved groundless. Commercial fishers are benefiting from having a protected cray and fish nursery in their backyard and in good weather the local waters are crowded with divers, snorkellers and glass-bottom boat passengers taking in the sights.

Goat Island Bay – a 90 minute drive from Auckland – has become one of the country's most popular beaches, attracting more than 100,000 visitors a year. In fact, due partly to the nearby Leigh laboratory, the reserve is probably the most dived and most investigated section of coast in the country. A four-year study by marine biologists – which alone involved 3000 diving hours – resulted in the publication of charts that identify 18 distinct habitats.

Thanks to the foresight of a few, busloads of children are now able to get close to marine life for school projects, hundreds of Jacques Cousteau wannabes wade into the water clutching disposable cameras and countless trainee divers learn how to fall off inflatables into an exhilarating underwater world.

The Marine Reserve includes five kilometres of coastline and extends 800 m offshore, providing plenty of room for the thousands of day-trippers. Visitors don't need to dive or snorkel to enjoy the underwater sights. A glass-bottom boat (top) or even just a wade through the rock pools (left) will open up a new view on the rich diversity of this marine wonderland.

Down on the Farm

Pakiri to Albertland

The area around Wellsford includes some prime dairy and cattle country. Here a farmer turns hay to allow it to dry for winter feed.

BELOW: The timeless ritual of moving the herd to the milking shed.

There is little sign now of early Maori occupation, or the Albertlanders who strove against all odds, or even the gumdiggers who spoiled these wide open hills. The landscape has healed and only the sounds of cows, skylarks, gently breaking surf and ghosts of the past ride the salty breeze.

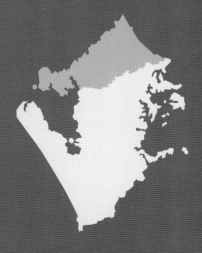

Pakiri Beach is one of the few stretches of undeveloped sandy coastline in the Auckland region. It affords a wonderful sense of space and solitude, as well as providing recreational opportunities, including surfing and horse trekking. The latter is sometimes accompanied by dolphins playing in the surf close to shore.

T HE WHITE SANDS of Pakiri Beach form a brilliant ribbon stretching north for 24 km from Pitokuku Reef near Goat Island to the spit of Mangawhai Harbour. The sand itself is, geologically speaking, a comparatively recent addition to this coast, much of it originating in the Taupo volcanic eruptions of 6500 years ago. It was carried through the Hauraki Plains and into the Gulf by the Waikato River – in the days when the Waikato went that way – and finally arrived at Pakiri to form the present beach and dunes.

The area was traditionally called Pakirikiri, and the name was further cemented in European times when the government granted Te Kiri the headland at the mouth of the Pakiri River around 1850. This land is the ancestral home of the Ngati Wai and the hapu Ngati Manuhiri. Shell middens from those times suggest that the sea was a generous provider of food. The land was generous too. In the heyday of timber-felling thousands of tonnes of kauri were floated down the Pakiri River and towed to Auckland. A timber mill ran for a time on ground now taken by a motor camp, and near the river mouth ships were built.

None of that industry survives, and for many kilometres the only movement these days, apart from the endlessly curling waves, is likely to be shimmering horses cantering below the pingao and spinifex. The horses will likely belong to Sharley and Laly Haddon who run Pakiri Beach Horse Rides, an award-winning tourist attraction that offers rides through forest and farmland and among the coastal hills and dunes. Visitors can follow an old warrior trail to freshwater lakes, retrace a kauri logging route, take a moonlight ride, or sign up for an overnight safari. Other options include a Maori hangi and taking part in a cattle drive.

The 2000 ha of coastal land on which the horses ride has never been out of Maori ownership. Laly, who has lived at Pakiri for 62 years, is part of a group of six extended Maori families who still live on the land left to them by Rahui Te Kiri. Their attempts at guardianship have on occasion led to disputes with the government, as when the families put up a fence to keep out four-wheeled traffic and disrespectful people. There have also been differences over boundary surveys and the financial pressure of rate rises.

It was heavy rates that drove the Haddons to develop horse trekking in the first place. The couple have 137 horses for trekking and Sharley breeds Arabian horses for endurance events. She also takes a keen interest in their history.

'Farming here is buggered,' says Laly bluntly. 'From the 1940s to 1956 there were 14 dairy farms – very economical units. But they've all gone. And very soon we'll be gone, because of the high valuation on the coast. If I had to rely on my sheep and cattle, they wouldn't even pay the rates.' The Maori Land Court, local authorities and regional councils have failed to acknowledge and address the historical significance of the Maori land at Pakiri, says Laly. In his view, the families risk being severed from it by financial debt while at the same time being hamstrung by zoning restrictions that limit their options.

It brings to mind the straitened circumstances of those who retired to Whangaparaoa Peninsula, only to find their fixed income won't cover increases in rates fuelled by escalating property values.

Pakiri, sandwiched between built-up Omaha to the south and Mangawhai, Waipu Cove and Langs Cove to the north, is one of the few relatively untouched beaches on the coast. Untouched, that is, apart from the barges that one year sucked 30,000 cubic metres of sand from the seabed just offshore for Mission Bay beach, and which take 200,000 cubic metres a year for the Auckland market.

'How can you fight that sort of destruction – that legal clout?' asks Laly.

He acknowledges that the families have done some residential developing themselves at Pakiri as a way of finding money for rates, but says their action is driven by necessity, not greed. 'I want Pakiri to remain a home for all Rahui te Kiri's mokopuna, because she fought so bravely against the government of the time to keep some land for us.'

Rahui Te Kiri and her husband Tenetahi were evicted from Hauturu, Little Barrier, in 1896.

Anyone who has spent a little time at Pakiri will understand the benefits of some form of protection. Oystercatchers and dotterel can sometimes be seen nesting in the dunes, and shags, pied stilts, herons, kingfishers and paradise shelducks in the estuary. Tuatua, horse mussels, trumpet shells, scallops and wheel shells often wash up on the beach. The generous kilometres of coastal forest, rolling dunes and foaming water have 'restorative' written all over them.

But Pakiri is also a place that fosters a different set of values. 'There's no such thing as a Maori or European up here,' says Daron Watene, who doubles as Rodney District ranger and Ngati Wai ranger. 'No one ever uses the words 'mine' or 'ours'. Sharing is what it is all about.'

The unsealed roads out of Pakiri churn to mud after rain and can concentrate the attention of travellers negotiating the hills. The high cost of hauling milk from local farms is one reason dairying fell away in these parts. Now, the fields here and in the backblocks north of Matakana, are full of beef cattle.

ABOVE: Every Tuesday at noon potential buyers look over stock at the Wellsford saleyards, which take sheep from as far as Dargaville and Kaikohe.

LEFT: Getting cattle and sheep to and from the saleyards was no easy task in the early 1900s; the much anticipated railway was still a stockmans' dream.

LEFT: Typical hard-won grazing land in the rural backblocks of Wellsford.

BELOW: An important event in the development of any rural town is the arrival of the railway. Wellsford Railway Station opened in 1909.

BOTTOM LEFT: Another load of logs is set to leave the Wellsford railway station. Each year Tranz Rail hauls about 60,000 tonnes from here to ports and mills around the country.

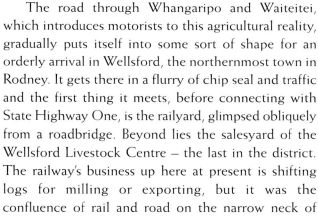

Untouched, that is, apart from the barges that one year sucked 30,000 cubic metres of sand from the seabed just offshore for Mission Bay beach

The road through Whangaripo and Waiteitei, which introduces motorists to this agricultural reality, gradually puts itself into some sort of shape for an orderly arrival in Wellsford, the northernmost town in Rodney. It gets there in a flurry of chip seal and traffic and the first thing it meets, before connecting with State Highway One, is the railyard, glimpsed obliquely from a roadbridge. Beyond lies the salesyard of the Wellsford Livestock Centre — the last in the district. The railway's business up here at present is shifting logs for milling or exporting, but it was the confluence of rail and road on the narrow neck of land joining Northland and the Auckland region that got the town going.

Port Albert, to the west, was to have been the hub of civilisation in this part of the country, at least in the fond imaginings of the nonconformists who settled there in the 1860s. Early on, however, several families decided to set up a satellite community on a saltwater creek some eight kilometres inland. Being a practical people, they pooled the first letters of their surnames to create a synthetic placename — Wellsford. More properly, Wellsford Creek. At this time the creek, a waterway to Port Albert and beyond, was their only practical link with the outside world.

By the turn of the century, Wellsford Creek was flourishing, with its own school, post office (in Mrs Rushbrook's house) and a local branch of the Port Albert cooperative store. Then, in 1909, tracks for the northbound railway were laid five kilometres east of Wellsford Creek and a railway station was thrown up on a windy fern ridge.

DOWN ON THE FARM

**Autumn is always a time of high drama
in the Warkworth Town Hall. There, on a day
in late March or early April each year, a crowd gathers,
judges don their white coats, contestants mount
the platform and 1200 sheep get nervous.**

A Cut Above
Northern Shears

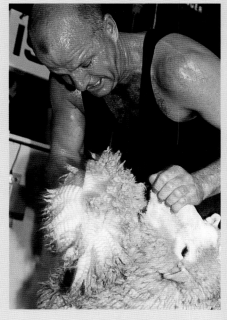

THEN, TO SHOUTED ENCOURAGEMENT and the buzz of electric shears, the black-singleted champions get down to business, slicing through thick fleeces and sending sheep down the chute.

The New Zealand Autumn Shearing Championship, one of half a dozen such events around the country, attracts not just top national and international shearers, but also local contractors and young teenagers keen to get their hands on one of the trophies.

The competition was planned over the dinner table 13 or more years ago by Ivan Rosandich, a competition shearer and judge who saw the need for something in the north which was of the stature of the country's premiere Golden Shears event.

Entrants are marked on speed, fullness of the cut and the quality of the finish on the sheep. The opinion of the sheep is not taken into account.

Apart from New Zealanders, the shearing championship attracts regulars from Australia and Britain, all vying to become the supreme champion and follow in the footsteps of David Fagan (above) who, until 1999, had won the Open Grade nine years in a row.

Wellsford quickly shuffled alongside the new iron road – or, rather, died in one place and sprang up in another. That done, it prospered.

Diehards lingered by the creek, but businesses there closed or relocated and soon even the church was on the move, tactfully coming to a halt a kilometre or so short of the new town. For a time there was uncertainty as to whether the highway north would favour the east coast or the agriculturally more productive, but in engineering terms more costly, Kaipara coast. Port Albert orchardists, meanwhile, tossed in their lot with shipping services, and for many years after the railroad came through, continued to freight their produce by water to Te Hana or down to Helensville rather than rely on the poor local road to Wellsford.

When the highway came, it pushed right through Wellsford's main street. These days passing motorists are barely aware of the place, unless they have business in town. For most travellers it is little more than a cluster of fast food outlets and petrol pumps on a hill, set amidst a rage of traffic.

Peak traffic count in Rodney Street is 15,000 cars, but Wellsford doesn't rank highly on Transit New Zealand's waiting list for bypass operations. It says a road diversion could be 20 years away, by which time it is estimated that the remaining coastal land nearby will become built out the way it has at Snells Beach. The completed Albany-to-Puhoi highway will drag Wellsford 10 minutes closer to Auckland by car, though it will still sit beyond most drivers' ideas of an acceptable commuting distance.

The town, nevertheless, is in good shape. Around 1650 people call it home, with up to 4000 more from as far afield as Oruawharo, Glorit and Tomarata using its commercial, financial and social services. It is predicted that even in 20 years places like Mangawhai with significantly increased populations will still took to Wellsford as a service centre.

One man to thank is entrepreneur Richard Izard, who started the saw-blade factory now called Izard Irwin International, which employs 270 people – soon to be around 400 people – and which pumps much-needed money into the local economy. It was while he was in the United States that Richard, a fifth generation New Zealander, 'and damned proud of it', stumbled on the technology that helped make Wellsford what it is – carbide tips. The hardened tips signalled an end to the labour of cutting timber with blunt blades, or of regularly taking time out to have them sharpened.

Recognising the need for high volumes to make manufacture of the blades practical in New Zealand, the company focused on export, winning a staggering 45 per cent of the world market – mostly in North America – and 85 per cent of the New Zealand market. To put that in perspective, filling New Zealand's annual orders is a morning's work for the company. Literally, one morning. The company also has a branch in Rotorua and subsidiaries in North America and Europe.

In 1991 Richard's company merged with another long-established New Zealand company and more recently was taken over by the United States manufacturer American Tool.

TOP: The Wellsford Trolley Derby started in 1997; two years later it attracted a crowd of 3000, almost twice the town's population.

MIDDLE: At Izard Irwin International tungsten carbide tips are sorted and welded onto saw blanks. Richard Izard (above) is the founder of this export-focused company that makes a significant contribution to the economy of Wellsford.

Te Arai Lakes (Spectacle Lake in the foreground, Tomarata Lake in the distance) offer a freshwater alternative to Pakiri Beach beyond the pine-forest barrier. They are also a favourite haunt of many waterfowl.

'I feel a little sad in some ways,' says Richard, 'but they made an offer we couldn't refuse.' Also behind the decision to sell was the fact that the existing company was dangerously reliant on a single product and that diversification would have cost in the region of $50 million.

The new company, Izard Irwin International, has shown what financial muscle can do by building an 800-sq m office and warehouse complex in Wellsford, with a second 2000-sq m building under construction to cope with anticipated future growth.

Richard, who now runs a farm five kilometres out of town, is a strong advocate of the road bypass, saying that once it happens Wellsford will rocket ahead. The place needs some entrepreneurial flair in retailing, including a supermarket, he says. 'Give us the bypass and that will come, if property development trends in the United States are anything to go by.'

Wellsford may have a bright future, but it has had its setbacks. One was the Great Fire of December 1955 that started in a stationer's basement and became an inferno, taking out two houses, four shops and a bank. Appliances arrived from Maungaturoto and Waipu, and the local brigade put up a spirited defence with a converted horse-drawn pump earmarked for a Reefton Museum.

Locals didn't let the fire get the better of them, though. Next day Bank of New South Wales staff opened for business in a rented main street building, using a safe brought up from Auckland.

Recently, the bank's successor, WestpacTrust, dented that goodwill by announcing the closure of its Wellsford branch, leaving the town with one ATM for locals, rural folk and passing motorists to fight over. And that ATM sometimes fails, forcing retailers to step into the breach and act as bankers

Old technology may not have been any more reliable, but it has a champion in Ray Treadwell, a publican forced to retire a few years back after a stroke. 'I had to find something to do, so I picked on phones,' says Ray, who now has more than 100 restored phones in his home museum.

The fabulous, deserted Pakiri
coastline south of Te Arai Point.
The 10-km forest, the heart of which
has recently been felled, was established
in the 1960s to check the drifting sands.

The collection's centrepiece is an 1890 Western Electric known as the 'twin box', powered by two glass battery jars and thought to have been used in the Port Albert post office. Ray found the phone by chance in an old Port Albert farm shed and spent six months restoring it. A stickler for detail, he even imported American walnut to match the original timber.

Other models include a 1930 skeleton phone, British and American wooden phones and the first set of dial phones issued by the New Zealand Post Office.

Ray's museum is in a street with pleasant rural views but cheek-by-jowl with modernity in the shape of a new subdivision. Its developers say the project, the first since the 1970s, ends a residential drought which has kept the town's population artificially low.

North of Wellsford, on a farm out of Te Hana and almost on the county line, sculptor Pat Foster has spent years avoiding town life altogether. Recently in the news for selling a 25-cm work in Nelson marble to Timaru's Aigantighe Art Gallery, Pat has fought hard for her success. Starting out as a science editor, she enrolled in an Elam summer school during her annual leave and there met John, her future husband. He brought her north to the 160-ha family farm at Te Hana but the first eight years were spent in a cottage at Mangawhai Heads.

'I had two daughters in that small place, so it was a struggle,' she says. 'And casting aluminium out at the beach was hair-raising.'

Pat is much taken by the teachings of the psychologist Carl Jung and describes herself as a Jungian sculptor. 'I trained as a psychotherapist part-time for five years but stopped when I reached the stage where I had to have clients. I thought, no, I'll be a sculptor.'

Her first piece after that decision depicted a bull being sacrificed. 'My ego, in Jungian terms. I was sacrificing my psycho-therapy.'

Pat works in a small shed behind the house watched, in a disinterested way, by Hereford steers. Beyond stands a woolshed, which John converted to a studio when the couple switched from sheep to beef, its two-storeyed interior a maze of partitions created by floor-to-ceiling murals.

The sheep may have made way for beef and art at Te Hana, but down Highway 16, just past the Port Albert turnoff and Hotea North, they reign supreme. There, on the flat, is Gordon Levet's Kikitangeo Romney Stud, the last big sheep property close to Wellsford. The farm itself dates from the 1870s when his grandfather broke in the land. In those days people journeyed from Wellsford to Port Albert or to Warkworth to catch the steamer.

'There was more agricultural land behind Wellsford than Warkworth even then,' says Gordon, now 66. 'Now the Wellsford stock sale is the only one left. It takes sheep from as far as Dargaville and Kaikohe.'

Massive changes have taken place since the boom times, sparked by the Korean War in the 1950s, he says. Then, a person could make a good living off 40 ha. Now people are scratching with 300 ha.

ABOVE: Pat Foster works from her studio on a farm at Te Hana. Husband John hangs his Technicolor murals in the woolshed out the back (top).

LEFT: Jim Jorgensen of the Wellsford Vintage Car Club stands beside his 1951 Chrysler at the annual swap meet, nowadays held at the Warkworth Showgrounds. Enthusiasts from all over the North Island mix with Wellsford's 50-plus members to buy, swap or barter anything from spare parts to the whole gleaming caboose. Eighty-year-old Jim still enjoys the big rallies in his pride-and-joy Chrysler which, he says, 'just loves those rough roads out the back'.

In September 1862, after a passage of 98 days,
a 954-tonne sailing ship, the *Matilda Wattenbach*,
entered the Waitemata with 352 people on board.
Among them were butchers, farmers, clerks,
drapers, millers, painters, wheelwrights, a farrier and
a glasscutter. They were the first of some 3000 settlers to
arrive in eight ships over the next two and a half years.
All bound for a place called Albertland.

THE ALBERTLANDERS
Port Albert

ALBERTLAND WAS THE PAPER CREATION of William Rawson Brame, the son of a Baptist minister, who hit on the idea of a nonconformist settlement after hearing of the establishment in Britain of a National Association for Promoting Special Settlements in New Zealand. A wily promoter, Brame sugared the scheme by naming it after the Queen's beloved consort, the late Prince Albert.

The nonconformists, regarded by many as second-class citizens, made landfall on the bicentenary of their expulsion from the Church of England, but their dream of a new start in the Britain of the South turned sour almost straightaway.

Instead of a bustling city, they found Auckland to be little more than a makeshift town, its buildings without spouting, and its streets and footpaths finished with rough scoria. Those who reached their allocated land found the journey to the upper Kaipara – by ship through the treacherous Kaipara Heads, or inland over boggy dirt tracks – difficult beyond belief.

Stepping ashore at their destination amid muddy estuaries and bleak fern wastes did little to raise the spirits. Marian Judson, whose family took two months to get from Auckland to Port Albert, wrote: 'There was a cluster of tents pitched on a small piece of comparatively level ground, which ran out into a point in the river. Low hills rising behind, half veiled in mist, and a drizzling rain . . . there was nothing to do but sit on a damp log watching the firelight. Such was our arrival . . .. Romance had faded into reality.'

'Deeds of heroism that will never be known were done daily by the turbid waters of the Oruawharo and Otamatea', one Albertlander was later to write. Many blamed Brame for their plight, and the best that can be said is that the 29-year-old visionary was defeated by the size of what he had taken on. Alienated by the migrants, he died in Auckland within a year of his arrival, having made just two brief and unhappy visits to Port Albert.

They came, they saw, they (were almost) conquered. Fighting droughts and food shortages, the settlers persevered, planting apple orchards and breaking-in pasture, though by 1880 it was clear that Port Albert itself was never going to grow into a town.

Today, more than a hundred years on, it remains an isolated huddle of houses on a headland. All-weather roads and the rise of dairying, eventually brought prosperity to the surrounding district, but the highway and the railway which helped open up the north ironically stimulated development in the middle of Albertland's waterless and windswept wastelands – a gumridge in the middle of nowhere, called Wellsford.

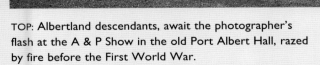

TOP: Albertland descendants, await the photographer's flash at the A & P Show in the old Port Albert Hall, razed by fire before the First World War.

ABOVE: Green fingers of land and muddy estuaries, mangroves, and rolling hills – Albertland has probably changed little since most of the Albertlanders moved on over a century ago.

LEFT: The Port Albert cemetery, where many of the early nonconformist pioneers lay at rest.

Such was our arrival . . .
Romance had faded into reality

The picturesque Minniesdale Chapel near Port Albert remains a solitary sentinel overlooking the Oruawharo River.

RIGHT: Harold Marsh ran a dairy farm at Wharehine until he died in 1948; he was also a gifted photographer as evidenced by these pictures of milking in the Marsh cowshed (above) and the drying of danthonia seed – a pasture grass – in 1919.

'I remember my uncle complaining that his new boots cost him one pound a foot. But lambs were fetching four pounds ten. These days boots cost $160 or more and lambs are worth $45.'

Gordon reckons most sheep farmers today spend 90 per cent of gross earnings on their farms – 'and would spend another 90 per cent, if they were looking after them'. Many cash-strapped farmers have to chase off-farm income, he says.

'One of my neighbours works at Sheepworld and, look, the gorse is coming back in.'

Gordon, former president of the Romney Association, puts the decline of sheepfarming down to three things: the unstoppable spread of Auckland, the comparative profitability of other types of agriculture and plantation forestry.

So Gordon is going into tourism – taking city folk round an authentic sheep property on trail bikes and telling the history of the place, how the bush was felled and the farm broken in. On the left there, the woolshed that took two men two winters to pitsaw back in the First World War. Here, some of the 4000 sheep and 400 cattle the farm supports. Up on Kikitangeo, the remains of Maori kumara pits.

Kikitangeo, which sits like a big grassy cone out the back of Gordon's homestead, is higher than just about anything on this coast north of Glorit and was last inhabited by Maori around 1830. The name, says Gordon, means either 'place of great weeping', or 'view of the Kaipara'. The last part is certainly true. From the summit big chunks of the Kaipara can be seen as well as snatches of the east coast.

From Hoteo North a side road, once a fairly useful cart track, winds out to Port Albert and the Okahukura Peninsula. It was at Port Arthur that Jane Mander, author of *The Story of a New Zealand River* and other colonial novels, spent time as a schoolteacher.

One of her characters, Allen Adair, talks of 'an exciting procession of events in the transmutation of bushland into prosperous farms, of isolation into settlement, of lonely tracks into railway lines'. But Mander herself

TOP: Albertland today: looking down the Oruawharo River towards the Kaipara Harbour.

ABOVE: In these parts, it seems, people either create things or collect them. Joan Greenfield collects salt and pepper shakers, hundreds of them, all matching pairs.

LEFT: Ken Auton lives in the remotest corner of Rodney District, not far from Mangawhai, and spends much of his time casting weta – as well as other iconic creatures – in bronze. The remarkable lifelike sculptures have given Ken a reputation that not only goes beyond Rodney's boundaries but beyond New Zealand's shores as well.

rebelled against what she called the 'brain-benumbing, stimulus-stifling, sense-stultifying, soul-searing silence' of provincial New Zealand. With that burst of angry sibilants she quit 'the barren wastes of Victorian Philistinism', writing most of her books in self-imposed exile.

Port Albert itself has changed little in the 130 or so years since the Albertlanders arrived from the English Midlands to make a fresh start. Some of the pioneers' proposed roads remain nothing more than lines on maps even today, though the settlers did soften the landscape with their pastoral pursuits and as a byproduct left several pretty buildings.

The well-kept Port Albert Hall stands on the road into the settlement along with Port Albert Church. Six kilometres further out on the peninsula is the Minniesdale Chapel, a delightfully modest vertical-board building set back from a picket fence on a hillside overlooking the Oruawharo River.

Further down the valley, beside a mangrove estuary, stands a house built in 1868. It was the birthplace of Enid Wiltshire, whose great grandfather, Rev Edward Brookes, was responsible for the chapel – his portrait hangs inside. In an admirable demonstration of forward planning he and his wife Jemima (Minnie) brought out the building's framing, glass, joinery and bell for the building, which was named after her. Many of the early Albertlanders, including the Brookes family, are buried in its cemetery.

Enid, who tidies the graves when she visits from Auckland, has fond memories of her childhood here.

'You could get a ship full of timber up to the house when I was young,' she says, looking at the mangroves that now grow on the silted inlet. 'It was nice and deep. You could swim there all the time.'

Enid lived in the chapel valley until at 18 she was forced to leave in search of work. Thinking back, she can find no cause for regret. 'It was the same everywhere. We didn't think it was hard, especially.'

It is the sort of hardiness that this part of the country was built on.

TOP: Another evocative Harold Marsh photograph, date unknown, of kauri gum being weighed in the Wellsford area.

MIDDLE: Apart from terns and gulls the lonely jetty at Port Albert gets few visitors these days.

ABOVE: Enid Wiltshire maintains her links with the area, ensuring the past is not forgotten.

The Land that Time Forgot

Helensville and the Kaipara Harbour

The Kaukapakapa River just north of Helensville, meandering to the Kaipara as if it has all the time in the world.

BELOW: Soft morning light and a slack tide conspire to give the Helensville waterfront an air of permanent tranquillity.

*A*t various distances within the heads, the rivers Kaipara, Tauhoa, Wairoa, Otamatea, Arapaoa and Oruawharo branch off in different directions, winding through some of the most fertile land in New Zealand, abounding with kauri and other valuable timber, and navigable for many miles.

THE NEW ZEALAND PILOT, 1958

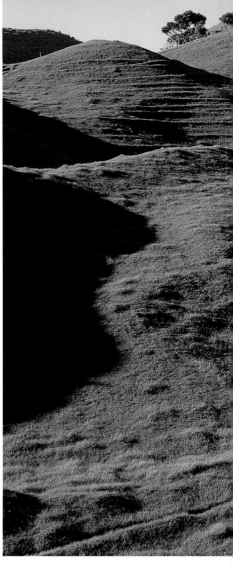

THE ROAD FROM WELLSFORD to Tapora on the Okahukura Peninsula points directly at the Kaipara's 6-km wide entrance until, running out of land, its nerve fails and it forks right and left. In each direction it tries to look busy but really has nowhere much to go among the grassed dunes. Anyone curious enough to venture this far winds up on a plinth of land smack in the middle of the biggest harbour in the southern hemisphere. To the north and south lie patches of water each the size of the Manukau.

The peninsula is named for Kahukura, a chief who came to the place some 600 years ago. He, or subsequent Maori, must have thought well of it because a great many archaeological sites have been found, suggesting solid occupation for generations.

In 1862 Ngati Whatua sold most of the peninsula to the Crown and a few years later Thomas Fitzgerald acquired it. He threw up a fence across the peninsula's narrow waist and farmed the land as one big cattle run. Kauri was logged by Helensville timbermen and the ground dug over for gum. Later the farm was carved into smaller holdings by the government as part of its post-Second World War settlement scheme for returned servicemen.

It is a delicate ecosystem here, and home to salt-tolerant plants including glasswort, paspalum and native lobelia. As in many other parts of the country, the native toetoe is losing out to the coarser South American pampas grass, but the birds still make a go of it. In late summer impressive numbers of godwits and knots congregate in readiness for their return to the Arctic.

Old-timers recall a bay near Orongo Point on the southern shore that once was black with wild swans and festooned with mussels hanging in thick clusters. Bert Staples, whose uncles leased a big block there, remembers staying in a cliff hut for a fortnight at a time in winter when the cows were dry. Now a perky 80-year-old, Bert talks of harpooning stingrays from a dingy and shooting snapper as, tails in the air, they burrowed for shellfish around Shag Roost Bay.

Then, says Bert, it was hardly possible to walk across the sandflats without treading on the eggs of nesting gulls and terns. He and his mates took the dogs out to hunt wild pigs that came out from the rushes to feed on the eggs. Today, the pigs are still in evidence, their tell-tale tracks lacing the sand.

Travelling in this corner of Rodney, from Tapora back to Wharehine and down to Tauhoa where the road joins State Highway 16, it is hard to imagine how difficult getting about was for the early settlers, the Albertlanders. In the beginning, their roads were just horse tracks roughly cleared of trees and, on boggy ground, strewn with fascines of timber and brush.

A lone mangrove on the Kaipara mudflats that seem to stretch for ever when the tide is out. A history of heavy logging in the district exposed the topsoil which then washed into the sea causing siltation on a massive scale, creating in the process an ideal habitat for mangroves to flourish.

LEFT AND BELOW: Behind the mudscapes and the indeterminate coastline, the rich Kaipara farmland climbs, dips and rolls in a succession of verdant patures. There was a time when forests dominated these tumbling hills; who would have thought that sheep would one day outnumber the trees.

One writer arriving in Port Albert in 1866 found no roads to speak of. 'The Government had built certain bridges, but the roads were not connected, and what there were might be described as "three feet wide and two feet deep".'

Unstable land and shifting foundations, along with a shortage of sealing metal, made roading around the Kaipara difficult and expensive. Then there were all the creeks and rivers to be crossed. The Minister for Works, Robert Semple, was moved in the 1930s to tell Cabinet that the roads in north Auckland were costing four times as much as the New Zealand average and were lasting half as long.

There was no all-weather link between Port Albert and Wellsford until around 1926, and the road to Wharehine wasn't metalled until almost 100 years after the first settlers arrived.

Breezing around the margins of the Kaipara today holds none of the terrors it did in 1917 when day after day a parliamentary touring party battled conditions which, even though it was January – the driest time of year – read like tag mud-wrestling on wheels.

ABOVE: The mail has to be delivered, even in the backblocks of Waitoki – a typical roadside scene in much of rural Rodney.

The fully-sealed and mud-free highway cruises south, keeping company with a coast which couldn't contrast more with the sparkling, embayed, deeply beached east and its island-studded vistas. Here, the road offers glimpses of water, mudflats and vast, recumbent headlands that seem to care nothing for anyone or anything. With a tide that drains half the harbour, leaving a series of flats each big enough to put a good-sized town on, and with endless shifts in perspective from the road, it is hard to fix the lie of the land.

This is better done from the aptly named Atuanui, or 'Great Deity', which, in pre-European times, was the mountain refuge of various Ngati Whatua hapu, whose earthworks are still visible. Less imaginatively renamed Mount Auckland by settlers, its summit is the apex of a rewarding 3.5 hour trek – the Mt Auckland Walkway – reached either from the highway a little north of Glorit, or from 3 km up the Kaipara Hills Road. The track winds through taraire forest filled out with nikau and the odd rimu, puriri, rewarewa and kahikatea. Side paths lead to groves of kauri.

The Atuanui State Forest, logged but spared the match, was given protection as a State Timber Reserve in 1887 and in 1963 a rare species of orchid, the tiny *Danhatchia australis*, was discovered here.

The view from Atuanui, Rodney District's highest point, is extensive. At its foot to the north is the biggest

TOP: A lone fishing boat reflects the sheer scale of the Kaipara Harbour.

ABOVE: Kaipara mudscape.

BOTTOM: Helensville was a busy place until the timber and gum expired nearly one hundred years ago, the population dwindling rapidly in its wake. But in 1958, when this photograph was taken, the main wharf looked as though everyone had abandoned the place only the day before. The town has still to emerge fully from its torpor. It won't happen overnight, but it will happen . . .

river in these parts, the Hoteo. To the east, Little Barrier Island is visible along with Whangarei Heads, while to the west stretches the flat pan of the Kaipara.

Some 10 km south of Glorit is Makarau where on Christmas Day 1886, to celebrate the rail track having got this far north, the good folk of Helensville and Auckland arrived by excursion train bound for Alfred Buckland's 4000-ha South Head Estate. At Glorit they piled aboard the SS *Kina*, and proceeded downriver to Buckland's wharf where they spent the day commenting favourably on the view and on the estate's bumper crop of potatoes and oats. They learned of wool shipments to England and of the impressive volumes of mutton and beef being sent to Auckland. It was all innocent good fun in an era when entertainment and the vogue for self-improvement often joined hands.

Travelling north any distance from Auckland in the middle of last century was an exercise in tenacity and forbearance. The best way was by boat across the upper Waitemata harbour to Riverhead, then by horse or bullock wagon over a rough road – once an old Maori trail – to Helensville.

A GRAND SCHEME
The Kaipara Railway

FROM THERE, BOATS JOURNEYED up the Kaipara Harbour to the northern Wairoa and set weary travellers ashore to strike out through the kauri forests to their final destinations. By 1869, settlers around Maungaturoto – south-east of Dargaville – had had enough. The practice of leaving their farms for 15 days at a time to take cattle to market, or shipping perishable fruit to Auckland via North Cape, had to stop. They pushed for a tramway linking the Waitemata and the Kaipara.

Auckland supporters added their voices and in 1875 the calls were answered with the opening of a rail link between Helensville and Riverhead. Six years later a line from Auckland reached the Kaipara railway at Kumeu and the short-lived section from Kumeu to Riverhead was closed.

Local Maori, who had generously gifted land for the tracks, found railway regulations vexatious, none more so than the requirement that fares be paid for the privilege of using the new-fangled transport. Some compensation, enjoyed by Pakeha and Maori alike, was that the lines made a convenient foot road.

By 1889 the line extended as far as Kaukapakapa, and early last century summer excursion trains hauled by small decorated engines were running to Parakai hot pools, while others took daytrippers from Helensville to the Ellerslie races, stock sales and A & P shows.

For many years the railway was the main employer in Helensville, but economic slump and the building of a main road north through the town eventually sealed its fate. There is one glimmer of hope: local enthusiasts, who now own the station, talk of restoring it and persuading Tranz Rail to run a needed commuter service.

ABOVE: The busy Helensville railway yards and wharf in the 1940s.

BELOW: The day the train went through the shed, 5 November 1913.

BOTTOM: In 1883 a vibrant Helensville could boast not just a railway but a flour mill and a timber mill, all contributing to its importance as the hub of the north.

In 1959 Helensville was an important service centre for the surrounding rural communities and shops like Screaton's Hardware had to stock all the necessities.

From Makarau the highway winds along with an increasingly busy feel, through the agricultural settlement of Kaukapakapa and alongside its river before flicking a corner or two and fetching up into Helensville.

Helensville squats against the Kaipara River at the southernmost tip of the harbour. It is a town that people either like a lot or accelerate through. One early visitor, P W Barlow, vented his dislike in the novel *Kaipara* (1889). 'The railway journey was decidedly uninteresting, the line passing through some most dreary looking country, which became more uninteresting as we neared Helensville, a township only impressive by its unsightliness,' he wrote. 'It stands on a river whose discoloured waters run between two banks of mud.'

From the river it is indeed something of a mess, scarred by rusting car bodies and the business end of commercial sites. But the place has a quiet appeal and more than its share of well-preserved villas dating from its late Victorian commercial peak. In fact, Helensville has the biggest concentration of heritage houses in Rodney District.

One of the country's most active ports in the late nineteenth century, it was an important railhead as well as being the terminus for coastal steamers. The town grew fat off gum, flax milling and, most importantly, timber. It was a timberman, John McLeod who, with his wife Helen, first settled here next to the Ngati Whatua village of Te Awaroa. Their family home, Helen's Villa, gave the future town its name. In the 1860s, McLeod's mill employed 100 men, and timber or squared logs were loaded into ships bound for the Waikato, the South Island, Australia and even further afield.

A freeze-frame of the frenetic activity of the port at its height can be got from the *Kaipara Times* of 13 February 1889. In its pages, the reader learns of the arrival of the barques *Wenona, Handa Isle* and *Bride.* The schooners *Frank Guy* and *Welcome* were then loading at the wharf and the barquentine *Parnell* had left with 215,000 feet of timber. The schooner *Yolande* was hard on its heels with 276,000 feet. Out at the Heads, the impressive *William E Witzeman*, which carried aloft more than 3000 square metres of canvas, had made its first entrance into the Kaipara.

An aerial view of Helensville and
the Kaipara River looking north.

CROSSING THE BAR
The Race for the Kaipara

On the Hokianga, in late December 1835, an extraordinary
contest developed between two headstrong Europeans that was to have
profound repercussions for the future of the Kaipara. One was a determined
Wesleyan missionary, the other an ambitious Irish timber trader
with a gift for colouring the truth.

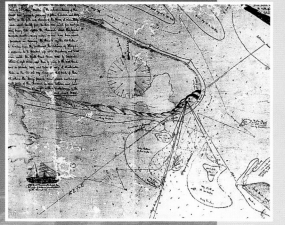

A chart of the entrance to Kaipara Harbour drawn by Captain Thomas Wing.

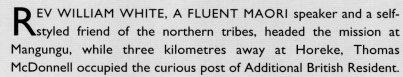

REV WILLIAM WHITE, A FLUENT MAORI speaker and a self-styled friend of the northern tribes, headed the mission at Mangungu, while three kilometres away at Horeke, Thomas McDonnell occupied the curious post of Additional British Resident.

McDonnell had recently returned to New Zealand after a visit to England where he had won both his novel appointment and a lucrative contract to supply spars to the Admiralty. With an eye on the vast and untouched kauri forests of the Kaipara, he promptly secured a large tract of land. There was just one condition: his vessel must be 'the first to cast her anchor in the Kaipara and to fly the British flag over her waters'.

The dream of entering the harbour — the biggest in the southern hemisphere — was not new. The missionary Samuel Marsden had made no fewer than three overland journeys to the Heads as early as 1820 to see whether ships might safely enter, but he hadn't reached any firm conclusion.

White, who also had commercial (as well as godly) designs on the Kaipara, got wind of McDonnell's plans around November 1835 and immediately chartered a ship himself. He intended discouraging the local chiefs from selling land and hoped, by beating McDonnell, to stop him fulfilling the terms of his contract.

Fortunately for White, the need to investigate a murder aboard a newly arrived schooner delayed McDonnell's departure and the missionary innocently slipped out of Hokianga ahead of him on 29 December aboard the *Fanny*. Two days later, hearing of White's destination, an alarmed McDonnell immediately flew after him aboard the *Tui*.

White later claimed to have got through the Heads first — on 6 January 1836, under the capable Captain Wing, who 'in entering the harbour crossed the outer sandbank, carrying three fathoms at high water, and worked out against a strong Westerly wind, by the middle channel'.

Brazen lies, said McDonnell. The *Tui* was already 'at anchor some 70 to 80 miles up the Wairoa . . . when the *Fanny* made her appearance'. Elsewhere, for good measure, McDonnell claimed to have sent the *Tui* through the Heads on 25 November 1835, while he himself was still in Horeke.

Wing, who drew up a detailed chart of the Heads, unhappily left off the exact date, and neither he nor Lawreston, captain of the *Tui*, had much to say either way. The increasingly strident claims and counterclaims of their employers, however, have left a bird's nest of contradictions which, at this distance, are unlikely ever to be resolved.

Whoever was first through the treacherous bar, in 1836 the history of the Kaipara was forever changed. Over the next 150 years many ships were to founder amid its shifting sands and storm-driven seas as yet another part of the country felt the bite of the logger's axe.

LEFT: It is not only the shifting Kaipara bar which has discouraged vessels for 150 years. Gradual silting of the harbour has created mudflats that have closed off many of the larger waterways.

INSETS: Two key players in the race for the Kaipara: Rev. William White (left) and Commander Thomas McDonnell.

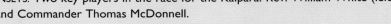

THE RACE FOR THE KAIPARA

Having taken their cargoes on board, ships were towed by steam tug to the harbour entrance, seeming to drift calmly above the mangrove flats as they went. Such were the serpentine meanders of the river that often two vessels heading downstream would appear to be travelling in opposite directions.

With the fall of the last kauri, Helensville settled down to become a service centre for the agricultural hinterland. Despite a renewal of timber milling with the start of plantation forestry in the 1930s, the town's role today is unchanged. The Kaipara Co-op Dairy, once its biggest employer, closed in 1988 and the building now marks time as a home to craft industries and a plastics manufacturer.

Helensville is home to many fine old buildings and the biggest concentration of heritage house in Rodney District. Historic public buildings include the Post Office (1911) and the Grand Hotel, built in 1930, after two previous wooden ones perished in fires.

LEFT: The annual Anzac Parade down the main street of Helensville.

BELOW: Kaukapakapa Library, established in 1865 and still going strong.

BOTTOM: In 1918 Helensville's Family and Shipping Butchery printed their own Christmas cards. Under this imposing photograph was their motto: 'Cleanliness and attention to business as usual'.

In the heart of Helensville, behind the new civic centre, sits the town's collective memory, the Helensville Pioneer Museum. Its collection of Maori and colonial artefacts and early photographs is housed in two adjacent buildings; a turn-of-the-century homestead and the splendidly preserved Helensville District Courthouse, built in 1864 using kauri from McLeod's mill. The courthouse, once used for sittings of the Maori Land Court, retains the trappings of those times, including judge John Rogan's chair. Hard-worked building that it is, it was still being used on its original riverside site as the District Courthouse until 1974.

Down the road towards the rail station is a barn-like deco presence called the Regent Theatre, which began life in 1941 screening ripping movies and newsreels of the European war. Now it is in the hands of arts aficionado John Perry, one-time director of the Rotorua Art Gallery. Born in the King Country, John arrived in Helensville in 1969 to teach art and after a time at the chalkface he took time out in Kaukapakapa – in 'a place without electricity,' he says, 'in the sanctuary of primeval forest.'

LEFT: A rainbow accentuates the wildness of the southern Kaipara's saltmarsh fringes.

Following the directorship in Rotorua, he is back and the Regent's windows are full of the fruits of his labours. Closed as a cinema since the early 1990s, it now houses in its cavernous interior an unbelievable pile of things – furniture, cases, china, boxes of kauri gum, framed pictures, folk art – all accumulated by John over 30 years. Some of it dates back to the days when he lived in a Newton Gully house and knocked about with Hamish Keith and Barry Brickell. 'Lootin' in Newton', he calls that era. Rich pickings.

'In my life chaos is the victor so often,' he says, standing among film memorabilia and stacks of unsorted old books in the Regent's foyer. 'It is a battle I wage daily.'

Having worked in a landmark building before, John wanted somewhere stylish for his collection. He found it in the Regent, which is in remarkably original condition – 'almost like buying a one-owner car'. His plans for the old cinema are ambitious: a theme café celebrating cinema history, a gallery, second-hand books, an area for antiques and collectables. But, then, he is an optimist when it comes to Helensville's future.

'At the moment this is the town that time forgot. No fast food franchise, no supermarket or service station with fluorescent welcome lights. But the nature of the place is changing. It is being dragged into the twentieth century.'

Yes, from the river Helensville looks like a set for Kevin Costner's movie *Waterworld*, admits John, but it is only 50 km from central Auckland. And it has a big thing going for it: its past. He offers a smile. 'It is a curious kind of junk heaven.'

'At the moment this is the town that time forgot. No fast food franchise, no supermarket or service station with fluorescent welcome lights.'

ABOVE AND RIGHT: To the north of Helensville is the relatively untamed South Kaipara Peninsula, where farming, forestry and wetlands combine with an increasing number of lifestyle blocks. Deer, too, have become a common sight on many farms.

LEFT: John Perry has great plans for Helensville's Regent Theatre, which at present houses his eclectic collection of film memorabilia, folk art and assorted artefacts.

The romance of rail is kept alive by steam enthusiasts offering special excursion trips, in this case between Helensville and Waimauku.

Councillor Arnold Gosling would agree. He heads a trust dedicated to restoring the town's historic rail station and getting the trains moving again. The trust, which bought the station building and the land it sits on, plans to reopen the tearooms and add appropriate paraphernalia to the site, including a footbridge it bought in Huntly.

At present, apart from steam excursion specials, the only trains coming close to Helensville station are freight wagons loaded with timber for northern mills. Passenger services ended in the 1970s, and one of the Council's stated objectives is to canvas Tranz Rail for a commuter service to Auckland. That would involve laying a double track to Helensville and investing in additional rolling stock, but Arnold believes the idea is sound.

The creation of affordable one-hectare lifestyle blocks close to the city has resulted in a ready demand for efficient public transport, he says. 'We strongly believe that when urban trains run again the station will have a commercial park-and-ride value as well as a heritage value.' In his view, it could happen within five years.

Helensville isn't a big place – 3000 people in Helensville/Parakai, and another 3000 in the rural hinterland – and it will never be big on industrial development, though it has begun to develop a stable workforce which is proving attractive for commercial operators. But, like other parts of Rodney, it is getting some population fallout from Auckland. Some locals predict Helensville ward's population will double in 5-10 years, though official estimates are more modest. It could do far more than double, though, if one of the options being considered by the Auckland Regional Growth Forum goes ahead: they are contemplating the effect of dropping a satellite city of 100,000 people in the area.

ABOVE: A Helensville success story: ex-dairy farmer John Burke of the boutique Burke's Brewery produces, in summer, some 1200 litres of beer each week, mostly consumed by the locals.

BELOW: Preparing for the next jump over Parakai.

BOTTOM: Peter McKenzie's fascinating collection of vintage farm equipment at Iron Park includes rare tractors, wagons and machinery dating from the 1900s.

Rautawhiri Park, a $2.6 million purpose-built sporting facility which opened in 1997, is perhaps a sign of things to come. The complex includes eight netball courts, eight tennis courts, four rugby and rugby league fields and an astrograss cricket pitch.

Another local recreational venue, the thermal resort at Parakai, 3 km across the river, continues to attract people who like their swims to be at a civilised 34 degrees. Started as a health spa, it was redeveloped into an aquatic park in the 1960s and now includes an even hotter indoor mineral pool and a hydroslide. Plans are underway to restore the resort to its former glory. This would be no mean feat. In the 1920s Auckland journalist Iris Wilkinson (the future Robin Hyde) declared that Parakai was a Reno, where visitors could gain a quick divorce from gout, rheumatism, lumbago and neuritis. A fellow visitor of the time swore that the caretaker at Parakai Domain stoked his furnace with the crutches abandoned by cured pilgrims.

Given the water's admirable properties, it is sad to relate the origin of the name 'Parakai'. In 1908 a Mrs Goad opened a private boarding house at the hot springs and the question arose of putting up a post office and giving the settlement a name – for years it had simply been called Helensville Hot Springs. A public meeting was called at which the favourite suggestion, Kaipara, was soon disqualified because of likely confusion with the existing Kaipara Flats. It seems that someone then suggested simply turning the word around. Kaipara. Parakai. And there it was. On a positive note, the unanimous decision to adopt the new name is, if nothing else, a salute to democracy.

There are other diversions in the vicinity, including solo or tandem skydiving at the Parakai Parachute Centre, or rather, from 10,000 feet above it. Then there is Te Pua's Iron Park, a museum of machinery including vintage and classic cars, early trucks and tracked vehicles, and household appliances.

Peter McKenzie, better known by the locals as Peg-leg Pete since an amputation in 1996 – the legacy of polio as a child – has assembled this unique collection over 40-odd years. At 65 he finds no greater pleasure than conducting visitors through the museum and sharing his encyclopaedic knowledge of his pet engines.

The missionary James Buller wrote of seeing near the Kaipara
'a vast sweep of silent and sombre woodland' in the 1830s, but the gaze
of less disinterested eyes had fallen on the northern kauri forests much earlier.
By the time Buller took in the view, traders had been active for years, floating out
logs as fast as the trees could be cut down, to help build Auckland and other
colonial towns and to satisfy the Royal Navy's appetite for masts and spars.

FRUITS OF THE FOREST
Timber and Gum

HALF A CENTURY LATER 'GOLD' FEVER struck the North as an estimated 20,000 prospectors poked, prodded and dug over more than 300,000 ha of land in search of kauri gum. The honey-coloured gum, harvested from living as well as long-dead trees and prized for varnishes and polishes, helped finance hard-working Croatians and other immigrants onto farms in the former gumfields north of Auckland. By 1885 much of the North, including a vast tract of land east of Helensville was being turned upside down for the hardened resin. In Helensville itself, notices were posted asking fortune hunters to refrain from digging in the street. That year, kauri and kauri gum accounted for almost 60 per cent of exports from Auckland province, much of it shipped through the Kaipara or railed from Helensville. In 1900 alone, 16 million feet of kauri timber left the Kaipara for Onehunga, southern ports and Australia, and more than 10,000 tonnes of gum was exported.

By the 1920s a growing scarcity of timber and the development of synthetic resins had eroded both industries and the scattered communities struggled to find alternative livelihoods. It was left to novelists like William Satchell to preserve a way of life which was rapidly disappearing. In *The Land of the Lost* (1902) he had written of the North's anarchic marches: 'In every direction the field stretches itself out to the horizon. . . . Once or twice a figure bearing an empty, or partially empty sack on its back, a spade across its shoulder, and a thin spear, shining like a splinter of glass in its hand, came into an open space and prodded the ground here and there . . . but no figure remained in view for longer than a few minutes at a time'.

Soon, they were to be little more than the playthings of memory.

Trees were felled all around the Kaipara, dragged to the water's edge and made into rafts. These rafts were known as 'herring-bones' which were then towed to the mills in Helensville. Later, when the land was laid bare, the gumdiggers moved in.

Back over the bridge into Helensville, among a stretch of roadside light industrial sites, is something that looks as if it has escaped from the Park – a Morris Minor clad in corrugated iron. This is the tell-tale property of metal artist Jeff Thomson, best-known for his corrugated elephants and farm animals. Out front and down the side of his workshop are stacked piles of old iron sheets in various stages of decay – what Jeff calls his 'library of materials'.

Jeff, who has been exhibiting since 1982, still makes his trademark sculptures to order but these days is often absent, working in overseas galleries as an invited artist.

Down at the town wharf, MV *Kewpie Too* offers regular sightseeing cruises, giving visitors the chance to make up their own minds about the river and, more importantly, getting them out onto the mighty Kaipara itself. Options include a two-day bus and boat trip with an overnight stop in Dargaville. A day cruise from Shelly Beach heads for the white sands of Pouto Point.

Shelly Beach is something of a hidden gem. At the end of a broad hook of land jutting into the harbour from South Kaipara Peninsula, it can be reached by road from Parakai, and on a still morning with a rising tide its handsome jetty is the perfect place to drop a baited line. Commercial fishers often land here with flounder netted on the harbour's generous mudflats.

Artist Jeff Thomson relaxes with a couple of his trademark sculptures in corrugated iron. He has even turned his car into a work of art.

In pre-European times the Kaipara was a foodbasket for the local Ngati Whatua, and is still regarded as one of the great New Zealand fisheries. At one time 30 or more boats dredged the harbour mouth for the mussels growing on the sunken logs and wrecks that were casualties of the timber trade. Mussel farming finally put a stop to the dredging business, though, and now half a dozen charter-craft fish the beds for snapper, trevally, kahawai, kingfish and gurnard. Seasoned fishers say this five kilometres of shoreline inside the bar, known as the 'graveyard' for its toll on shipping, is one of the best in the harbour, but its strong currents often make demands on people and boats. The bar itself runs out more than 20 km from North Head and 80 per cent of the Kaipara empties through here twice a day. Where an outgoing tide meets determined Tasman rollers it can throw up 15-m waves.

TOP: At the end of the wharf at Shelly Beach is a safe channel for larger vessels to follow in between the mudflats and mangroves of the southern Kaipara.

ABOVE: The best way to explore the tricky waters of the Kaipara is aboard one of the boats offering regular sightseeing cruises.

Little known Lake Karaka, like so many of the
dune lakes on the peninsula, is a haven for wildlife.

Beyond the protective curve of Papakanui Spit, the South Kaipara
Peninsula is home to varied outdoor pursuits including, surprisingly,
freshwater fishing. Within the past 6500 years a string of dune lakes has
been formed by a build up of sand ridges behind Muriwai Beach, and these
came to be known by local Maori as Nga Tapuwae o Kawharu, 'the footprints
of Kawharu', for a famous ancestor. The lakes now support introduced coarse
fish including rudd, tench and perch as well as freshwater crayfish (koura).

The largest and most northerly lake, Ototoa, is favoured for trout fishing.
It fringes the peninsula's largest tract of indigenous forest, and is a significant
habitat for native birds including grey duck, New Zealand scaup, shoveler,
bittern, fernbird and shags. Other lakes, including Kereta, are popular with
coarse fish clubs, as are some private dam ponds on nearby farms.

This part of the country has attracted a few wild schemes including a
plan to drain the Kaipara for dairying and, in the 1970s, a short-lived plan
to put a nuclear power plant on Oyster Point. In 1920 an idea was hatched
to push a rail line to Shelly Beach, which unlike Helensville was not reliant
on tides, and build a port there. Understandably, townsfolk got riled at the
thought of losing shipping and being bypassed by the railway. To many
people's relief the Waterways Commission declined the proposal, and it was
later learned that silting due to land clearing had badly affected the harbour
entrance, all but sealing it to big vessels. Nor did anything come of John
McLeod's long-cherished and often revived idea of a canal linking the
Waitemata and the Kaipara – the 'Mediterranean of the South', as some
called it who must have averted their eyes before the tide fell.

This part of the country has attracted a few wild schemes including a plan to drain the Kaipara for dairying

Further north lies
picturesque Lake Ototoa,
once the site of a Maori pa.

Visitors to the MacNut macadamia farm at South Head are welcome
at any time, but the best time to see the trees in flower is October-November.

Less fancifully, the peninsula is also home to the country's first large-scale macadamia farm. Started on a converted 40-ha dairy farm, its 1100 trees produce more than 20 tonnes of the sought-after nuts each year. Grafted trees are available at the farm, along with macadamia confection, cooking oil and cosmetics. Visitors can also take a tour of the garden, lakeside walks and orchard, and ponder the trees that concoct the world's toughest shells.

A few kilometres further out toward South Head, up a long pleasing drive banked with sandstone, lives the last person anyone would expect here – former Ceramco boss Sir Tom Clark.

'Trish and I decided to get out of Auckland and shift into another gear,' says the 83-year-old Sir Tom. 'Last-the-distance mode.' That was 20 years ago, and almost single-handedly he has transformed a three-hectare chunk of the property – which at one time totalled 600 ha – into a garden of delights.

Sir Tom, who before shifting here had never planted a thing in his life, isn't about to throw in the trowel yet, either. From 8 a.m. to 5 p.m. most days he is out planting and trimming, adding to his gallery of plants. But, finally, he is getting the better of the land. 'This is the first year I've had time to wander around and enjoy it.'

When he first arrived, Sir Tom ran cattle, then switched to fallow deer. Another deer farm, Waioneke, in its day the North Island's biggest, was just four kilometres up the road. When the market crashed Sir Tom got out of deer and cut back the size of his farm.

Sir Tom Clark in his garden, enjoying the fruits of his labour.

'The thing that gets me about the place is its tranquillity,' he says, lowering to a worn garden seat. 'I used to come out as a lad shooting deer. But I never thought for a minute this is where I'd end up.'

If it can happen to Sir Tom, it can happen to anyone. The Kaipara has that sort of pull.

ABOVE: Spring grass covers the rolling dunes of South Head. In the distance the notorious bar obstructs the harbour entrance – the Graveyard – while beyond, lies the Kaipara's North Head

LEFT: Carcases litter the northernmost dunes at South Head where, every so often, New Zealand's Armed Forces put derelict vehicles in the firing line.

LONG ROAD
TO THE FUTURE

WOODHILL TO RIVERHEAD

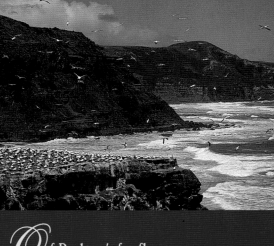

O'Neill Bay, Erangi Point and Bethells Beach – a long way from home. Unless, of course, you're lucky enough to live there.

BELOW: Gannets swirl above Motutara Island at the south end of Muriwai Beach.

Of Rodney's far-flung corners – Whangaparaoa Peninsula, Te Arai, Okahukura Peninsula, South Head and Bethells Beach – the latter is surely the most remote. So out on a limb is it, further south in fact than Auckland's Queen Street, many think of it as belonging to somewhere else. Yet it sits, wild and resplendent, in the most diverse of the District's rural quarters, rich in market gardens, nurseries and vineyards.

To TRAVEL FROM HELENSVILLE south towards Auckland is to go against the flow of history. The present Highway 16 makes short work of it, keeping company with the rail track as it powers through the valleys used by the Kaipara and Kumeu Rivers.

Old North Road, a shadow route a few kilometres to the north which began life as a simple walking track, was built with its notional arrows going the other way. In settler days it conveyed supplies from Riverhead at the western tip of the Waitemata to Helensville, then a buoyant timber town, and it sometimes managed to get timber back to Riverhead – at least until the more efficient railway was completed in 1875. Hopeful immigrant families, leaving Riverhead in bullock wagons or on foot, also took the road to Helensville, punctuating what was an arduous journey with roadside camps. Once at Helensville they boarded boats bound for virgin lands – and often heartbreak – beyond the Okahukura Peninsula. Such was the chaos of those days that new arrivals sometimes had to mark time for weeks on the banks of the Kaipara River while a suitable boat was built.

Riverhead in the mid-nineteenth century was a surprisingly active settlement. Briefly considered as a possible site for Auckland until Governor Hobson thought better of it and raised the flag on Point Britomart, its prominence as a transport hub nevertheless helped it attract sizeable manufacturing projects. It was helped by having a riverside location suited to waterwheels, with plentiful fresh water and all-tide access.

In 1845 Erasmus Brereton built a timber mill there and it ran for more than a decade before being replaced by John Brigham's Waitemata Flour Mill. That mill, in turn, was relocated to Fort Street and in the 1890s the Riverhead site was home to New Zealand's biggest paper mill. It produced the stuff which carried the news of the region until the First World War.

Waimauku has become the flower-growing 'capital' of Rodney, with sunflowers, narcissi, irises and carnations all grown extensively for the Auckland market.

INSET: Having served its purpose a long-retired tractor is left to rust away in a forgotten corner.

BELOW: One of the beautifully preserved mill-workers' cottages still standing in Riverhead.

ABOVE: It's not a flood exactly but the Kaipara River, near Woodhill, will usually top its banks after heavy or persistent rain.

FAR LEFT: The old Riverhead hotel, now known as the Forester's Arms, was built in 1875 – the second oldest continuous licence in the land. This photograph was taken in 1924.

BELOW LEFT: Riverhead's paper mill started production in 1898 and ceased in 1923 when much of it was dismantled and shifted to Southland; once there, Riverhead's newest machinery was used to restore Mataura's oldest.

LEFT: The Auckland to Kumeu double-engined Fairlie locomotive known as 'Snake', posing at Riverhead in the mid-1880s.

Pinus radiata as far as the eye can see. Each year about 350 ha of Woodhill Forest is cut down, yielding close to 200,000 cubic metres, nearly two-thirds of which is trucked to North Island sawmills, the rest exported — just some of the information being enthusiastically absorbed by this group of school visitors.

BELOW: The Kauri Gum Store, museum and café, Riverhead — still selling gum after 140 years. Consider it a good buy at $2.50 per 25 grams.

Nothing much remains of all those industrial goings on now, though building rubble and the vestiges of a water race and boat landing can still be seen down on the foreshore where Highway 18 — which has to be one of the shortest highways in the country — crosses the Rangitopuni Stream. The scrappy public reserve has the feel of a place biding time until its accomplishments are rediscovered, though what might happen there is anyone's guess. In nearby Elliot Street stand four well-preserved mill-workers' cottages, while further along is the ageing but well-patronised Forester's Arms Tavern, which dates from 1876.

The stream itself preserves the pre-European name for Riverhead. Rangitopuni, 'day of the dogskin cloaks', harks back to a peace agreed there by Ngati Whatua and Te Kawerau in the eighteenth century. Europeans began staking out land in the area in 1844, digging and trading kauri gum in Riverhead around the turn of the century and in the 1920s even harvesting tobacco – 'Riverhead Gold'.

The Kauri Gum Store (1860), now relocated to

School Road, served the local diggers and for the first 20 years of its life was near the mill. Present owners Tony and Ianthe Taylor, who took over the historic store in 1977, still trade in gum, several boxes of which stand in a corner. It is getting hard to come by these days, though, and espresso coffee and country cooking are what bring most customers through the door.

While in the neighbourhood, city folk often take the opportunity to poke about the local real estate offerings. 'A lot of people are wanting to get out here now,' says Tony. 'Riverhead is only 20 minutes from Ponsonby Road.'

The settlement is unlikely to run out of room to breathe. At its back is the 3800-ha Riverhead Forest, which was first planted before the First World War when the land was found to be too sour and poorly drained for farming. Aerial topdressing improved matters considerably and now forest manager Carter Holt Harvey makes a living growing pine and eucalypts here and at the bigger Woodhill Forest shouldering Muriwai Beach.

Woodhill is the first thing of any substance that Highway 16 meets after leaving Helensville. Much bigger than Riverhead, at 12,500 ha all up, it is also more recent, having been planted in the 1930s to slow the inland march of coastal dunes.

A little further on from the Woodhill Forest information centre is a modest sign on a well-used private side road advertising sand for sale. The sign belongs to David Steele, who farms sheep and cattle here on 100 ha. Once there were big deposits of sand under the grass at the back of the farm, but in 1942, with most local sand lost to forestry, an earlier owner opened a pit and sand was carted off by the truckload to fill sandbags at the Devonport naval base. Construction of the Northwestern Motorway took more and eventually David, who bought the property in 1962, negotiated a licence to extract sand from forest land.

ABOVE: In 1923 the National Tobacco Company was formed and Riverhead tobacco, under the brand name of 'Riverhead Gold', became a household name.

LEFT: Woodhill Forest is leased from the Crown by Carter Holt Harvey which purchased the rights to harvest and manage the forest in 1990. The forest cycle — from planting to clear-felling — is nowadays a mere 27 years.

If you go down to the woods today – at least,

if you go to Woodhill Forest – it will quite likely be to

hunt fallow deer, race motor bikes or to go horse trekking.

Or you may simply be there, like thousands of others

thoughout the year, for a pleasant stroll and a picnic.

A TEDDY BEAR'S PICNIC

Woodhill Forest

MORE THAN 100 CLUBS AND GROUPS devoted to activities such as orienteering, cross-country running, mountain-biking, paintball games and endurance horse riding regularly use the forest, helping push visitor numbers for this popular tract of land to more than 500,000 a year. The forest is given an injection of sword-and-sorcery whenever the makers of the longrunning television series Xena shoot a scene among the trees, while on the peninsula's northern tip airforce pilots regularly indulge in their own brand of outdoor pursuit above the Ministry of Defence's Air Weapons Range.

A former State forest, Woodhill has been managed since 1990 by Carter Holt Harvey, which each year clear-fells about 350 ha of radiata pine from the 12,500-ha forest. Some 60 per cent of the harvest is trucked to local mills and the company's Kinleith paper mill, with most of the balance exported to China and Korea.

Woodhill is only 35 minutes from downtown Auckland and as one of the closest forests to a major population centre warrants the title 'urban forest'. Aside from recreation, it is heavily used as an educational resource by primary and secondary schools and by tertiary institutions.

Carter Holt Harvey has recognised the importance of Woodhill by taking the unusual step of building an on-site education centre staffed by an educational programme coordinator.

Visitors to the centre may be surprised to learn how different the forest once was. When missionary Samuel Marsden passed through in 1820, the kauri forests had already succumbed to natural fires or to clearing by local Maori, and he recorded seeing 'high sandhills without vegetation upon them – several miles broad'. In the 1870s settlers compounded the problem by burning off the bordering bracken and manuka to make pastures, and sand drifts soon spread over newly won farms. When the vital rail link north through Helensville was threatened, action was at last taken.

Depression-era labour was put to work planting lupin seed and French marram grass to help stabilise the land and in 1936 planting began of Monterey pines – later to be known as *Pinus radiata*. The pines were so successful that in 1951 the New Zealand Forest Service began to run Woodhill as a production forest. Surplus military equipment from the North African campaigns of the Second World War, including Bren gun carriers and trucks, was found to be ideally suited to local conditions and soon they were churning their way to yet another desert victory.

Woodhill Forest is in strong demand throughout the year for recreational activities. Facilities include an off-road motorcycle arena, a scenic drive, walking tracks, barbecue and picnic areas and access to Muriwai Beach. Visitors can enter the forest at three points: Woodhill HQ, Rimmers Road and Tasman Road close to South Head.

'We got into quarrying as a sideline,' says David, whose son works a front-end loader at the sand-face a few hundred metres from the house. He estimates 100,000 cubic metres a year heads out the farm gate to be used for concrete roof tiles, bricks and roading hotmix. Some is earmarked for filling the new gasline being laid to Helensville.

David Steele is Rodney District Council's longest serving councillor, having represented Kumeu ward for 25 years. The experience – along with that of his father, who was a councillor when Kumeu was part of Waitemata – has left him with strong views about what is best for the area.

Some residents out Helensville way are in favour of being run from Waitakere, saying they have more in common with people on this coast than over on the east coast. David will have none of it.

'Waitakere wants to take us over but I'd prefer that we stayed with Rodney. Originally, we were in Waitemata and we fought hard to get out of the city area.' High rates, he says, would ruin the local farmers. 'That's why there is no farming at Bethells.' Even the current regime is tough, he adds, with little profit from the land except in dairy. 'Even dairy is getting down now. Paying $10,000 to $15,000 in rates. It's too much.'

David admits the low rating base is a big problem in Rodney because the District still has a long way to go with such things as roads, sewerage and water. Laly Haddon up at Pakiri would no doubt nod at the word 'problem', but a little way down the road from the sand quarry is someone who has helped put a new urgency into talk of land.

The low rating base is a big problem in Rodney because the District still has a long way to go

Margaret Kawharu lives in a kauri villa on a ridge near the Whiti Te Ra Reweti marae where, until a new one can be built, a temporary structure serves as a meeting house. On the walls of her home are heavily framed photographs of her forebears. Cradled in her arms as she talks is her baby son Zen Te Hikoi. She tells something of the history of the place: how the land she is on is a small part of Pukeatua Block, itself one of a number of parcels of family land hereabouts derived from her ancestor Paora Kawharu.

As manager for a land claim lodged with the Waitangi Tribunal by Ngati Whatua o Kaipara ki te Tonga – Southern Kaipara Maori – Margaret is well-versed in the grievances of local Maori. Five of Rodney's six marae are involved in the Southern Kaipara claim: Reweti; Haranui (Parkhurst); Te Kia Ora (Kakanui); Te Aroha Pa (Araparera); Puatahi (Glorit).

Muriwai is not all sand, surf and wide open spaces. Behind the beach there are several remnants of native bush that have survived the salt-laden westerlies, the self-seeding pines and encroaching homes.

LEFT AND ABOVE: 'Sand For Sale'. David Steele's sand extraction business is still shifting the stuff by the truckload – and there's a whole lot more where this comes from.

BELOW: Steps over the bluff at the southern end of the beach lead to Maori Bay, also accessible around the rocks at low tide. The high route is, however, the recommended one, with superb views of distant Oaia Island and the nearby Motutara Island with its famous colonies of gannet and tern.

She says a trigger for making the claim, which involves 17,000 ha centring on Crown-owned Riverhead and Woodhill Forests, was a Court of Appeal case over State-Owned Enterprises in 1987 which ruled that claims must be resolved before such land could be sold. Ngati Whatua felt that selling the SOEs in the case of Woodhill would jeopardise ancient burial grounds, traditional food gathering places and historically important sites.

Two years before the Court of Appeal case the Treaty of Waitangi Act had been amended to hear disputes dating back not just a decade but to 1840. That opened the floodgates, allowing examination of a deep-seated belief among Ngati Whatua that the Crown broke an unwritten partnership, an 'alliance', which their forebears forged at the beginning of European settlement.

'In the 1840s Ngati Whatua had formed a partnership with the government which had strong mutual benefits including the development of markets, education and medicine,' says Margaret. 'Ngati Whatua were very involved with the early governors and gifted land for rail and for a courthouse at Helensville. In return they looked to the Crown to offer development and infrastructure to the iwi of the region. But by the 1860s it was clear that our leaders were not going to get much equality.'

The four-hectare block donated for the courthouse by Te Otene Kiko-kiko in 1864, part of which was turned into a public park in 1924, was in the 1990s the subject of Rodney District's only occupation protest by Maori.

Claimants argue that Maori alienation from the land around the Southern Kaipara – they lost 97 per cent of it after 1840 – led to impoverishment and a dependence on wage labour and social welfare handouts. In the words of legal counsel Grant Powell: 'People who live just up State Highway 16 from Auckland were born in houses with mud floors and sacking for walls.'

The basic goal of any claim on Crown land, says Margaret, is to reverse the situation by gaining a solid economic base for the future. That, along with reaffirming the place and mana of local Maori. 'Recognition for our sense of place and guardianship over the land is something we feel we struggle with all the time.' In that connection, claimants would also like to see Helensville renamed Te Awaroa in deference to 300 years of settlement by Ngati Whatua.

. . . selling Woodhill would jeopardise ancient burial grounds . . .

Looking north along the rugged coastline from Raetahinga Point, between Bethells Beach and Muriwai. Pasture is gradually taking the place of the stunted manuka on these windswept headlands.

Muriwai, known traditionally as One Rangatira, 'the Chiefly Beach', is one of those places that can humble a person.

THE SAND HIGHWAY
Muriwai Beach

LEFT: The gannet colony at Muriwai is reputed to be the second most popular tourist attraction in the Auckland region. The colony is home to over 2000 birds and slowly increasing.

INSET: And the same can be said of the fishermen who also compete for space.

BOTTOM LEFT: Less conventional vehicles, like this sand yacht, are regular users of the highway that is Muriwai Beach.

BELOW: Going or coming? The scale of Muriwai Beach is graphically illustrated by the lone vehicle racing against nightfall.

ONCE CLEAR OF THE SMALL SETTLEMENT that anchors its southern extremity, determined walkers are soon swallowed up by the sheer immensity of the beach – more than 48 km of wave-washed sand dissolving into haze. Trekking through it can give the illusion, despite hours of hard effort, of being pinned to a ribbon of ground and subjected to the pounding of recycled surf and blasts of ozone-rich air.

Few people make the two or three day journey on foot to Papakunui Spit and South Head. One of the earliest Europeans to bend his legs for any distance in that direction, the missionary John Butler, was driven by hunger and thirst amid the immense tract of barren sand and whirling wind to meditate on the 42nd Psalm 'As the deer panteth for the water brooks. . .'.

Those who venture north these days usually do so in cars and off-road vehicles, hundreds of which churn the sand every summer – the beach is a designated public road to South Head. Conservationists blame such traffic for the demise of the toheroa shellfish, now fully protected. Others question the decision to allow vehicles to use the southern end of Muriwai, New Zealand's most popular surf beach.

Most people content themselves with less controversial recreation, line fishing off Flat Rock, horse trekking, playing the sandy fairways of Muriwai Golf Club's 64-ha golf course or visiting the gannet refuge at Otakamiro Point. Terns nest on cliff ledges here, and in spring fur seals can often be seen basking on the rocks below.

To many, the star attraction is the gannet colony. These lively sea birds nest in spectacular fashion at the southern end of Muriwai beach on outlying Oaia Island, on a narrow offshore pillar of rock called Motutara and, more recently, on the headland itself. The spread of the breeding colony, the most accessible and most northerly of New Zealand's three mainland colonies, prompted the establishment in 1979 of a takapu refuge.

Now, visitors can study the sleek birds at close range from a clifftop viewing platform. They begin nesting in late July and by mid-November the colony is humming with more than a thousand birds at home or wheeling over the ocean, where they dive from impressive heights for fish and small squid.

Most chicks leave for Australia at four months, returning when they are three to seven years old to build seaweed and guano nests like their parents did, just beyond striking range of angry neighbours.

The effect on Maori of Crown purchases to the west of Helensville for sand dune reclamation can readily be seen in a visit to Muriwai Beach. The beach was once heavily inhabited and the remains of fortified coastal pa can still be identified. One of the most formidable was Korekore, known locally as Wharekura, and still visible from all of Muriwai. Without access to the beach, they were effectively cut off from an important source of food. Today, a signposted road leads from Waimauku to the Muriwai settlement and getting among the waves is no longer a problem. Fishers intent on landing something for the table try their luck with surfcasting rods from places such as Flat Rock, a wave-swept ledge overlooked by the headland gannet colony. Old stories tell of moa being hunted here into the mid-seventeenth century and the traditions of Ngati Te Kahupara refer to moa as Te Mana Pouturu, 'the bird on stilts'. The time of catching the flightless creature has long passed, as have the more recent days of harvesting succulent toheroa from the yielding sands. From an estimated 10 million in 1964, the toheroa population declined to around 100,000 in 1986, despite protection efforts including, from 1976, a total ban on gathering the shellfish.

Some blame climate change and a lack of food, while others point the finger at the increasing presence of vehicles on the beach. Over a weekend at the height of summer, it is not unusual to see upward of 800 off-roaders driving over the beds; for reasons that aren't entirely clear, Muriwai Beach remains a designated road.

The road to Muriwai had been open since 1916, though as late as 1928 the journey was described by the *New Zealand Motor Journal* as very likely unequalled in the country for discomfort. The first motorist to head onto the beach itself was William Jones, a local farmer who got sand under his tyres in 1918. Unhappily, his tyres became too well-acquainted with the sand, and he suffered the ignominy of being pulled out by horses. After the First World War, the beach became a popular venue for motor racing, the first contest taking place in March 1921. A warning included in the first printed programme advised spectators to stand clear of the racers. 'At 50 mph, even with good brakes, a car takes at least 250 feet to pull up,' they were told. Helpful hints were included on general motoring: 'Don't drive too slowly on an open road. Fifteen to twenty miles an hour is the most economical speed, everything going with a nice swing . . .'.

In 1925, despite an overnight gale which played havoc with tents, a crowd of some 6000 enthusiasts assembled to watch a championship race which had attracted entrants from as far as Australia. They were treated to the spectacle of a successful attempt on the 100 mph speed record. The record was broken by a Sunbeam which needed all of three miles to get up speed. The driver, William Hamilton, a later pioneer of adventure tourism gained fame as the developer of the Hamilton jetboat.

Muriwai's days as a racing venue were numbered though – rough roads, troublesome tidal rips near the track and problems of crowd control soon saw motorsport shift to a purpose-built speedway near Mangere, a much less challenging destination for city folk.

TOP: A million mussels, temporarily stranded on a rock shelf at Maori Bay, wait for the incoming tide.

ABOVE: A lone fisherman on Flat Rock, braving the huge waves in the hope of hooking something bigger.

LEFT: Black sandy dunes and toetoe merge with the distant haze of Muriwai's 48-km beach.

ABOVE: Gathering irises on the Altorf farm, Waimauku.

BELOW: Black swans on the Bethells Swamp, a real haven for wildlife.

BOTTOM: O'Neill Bay from the Te Henga Walkway, looking south towards Bethells Beach.

With the demise of car racing, visitors to Muriwai slipped into an easy routine of surfing, swimming and fishing they still enjoy today. Muriwai is New Zealand's most popular surf beach, though deceptive rips and rogue waves each year claim the lives of swimmers and fishers. Horse riders skirt the fringes of the sea and golfers play on the spectacular fairways of Muriwai Golf Club. Further up the beach, land yachts can sometimes be seen resurrecting the excitement of motoring's early years.

A little further south, at Bethells Beach, Te Henga Walkway begins. It is a nine-kilometre trail leading visitors past sites of significance in the coast's early history including the place of the original Maori village of Waiti, O'Neill Bay, named for the first Pakeha settlers here. There is also an old track known poetically as Te Ara Kanohi, 'the pathway of the eye', for the superb vistas it offers as well as the remains of several headland pa. En route, walkers pass through regenerating coastal forest and along cliffs before the track takes them out through farmland.

It is possible to deviate from the Te Henga Walkway to Goldie Bush, a 190-ha chunk of regenerating forest donated to the people of Auckland after the death of timber merchant and former mayor David Goldie in 1926. A path leads to Mokoroa Falls, named for a taniwha said to live in the pool below the cascading water.

A few kilometres off is Bethells Swamp, which started life thousands of years ago as a lake when creeping dunes blocked the Waitakere River and the Mokoroa Stream. More recently, heavy logging caused silting and created the present 80-ha wetland – one of the region's biggest. Among the birds seen here are bittern, fernbird, spotless crake, banded rail and the ubiquitous pukeko.

Just off the Muriwai Road as it strikes out for the coast from Waimauku is the property of Peter and Joan Altorf. Their thing is irises – and they have 14 ha of them. The couple import the bulbs from Holland by the temperature-controlled containerload and from January workers plant out 200,000 a week. As a result, the Altorfs supply the New Zealand market with eight to 10 million stems a year. The numbers are big, but even so, growing flowers can be a gamble. This year two containers' worth of bulbs were lost to heat damage after being planted out and now more are succumbing to disease.

'We've been on this land 30 years,' says Peter who emigrated from Indonesia in his 20s. 'And we are still struggling.'

A lot of produce comes off this plateau though. The land is fertile and relatively frost-free, though the wind can get up. Down the road are growers of chrysanthemums and carnations. Francis Brothers export foliage for flower arrangements. Graham Franklin, nearby, specialises in celery. Then there are peppers, fruit, other vegetables – some signalled by roadside stalls. And everyone gets on well. 'All neighbours and mates.'

'The weird thing is people don't move,' says Joan. 'And when people do shift they end up

TOP: Mokoroa Falls, a dual attraction in Goldie Bush. Access is from Horseman Road via Waitakere or Constable Road, off Oaia Road, 10 km down the Muriwai road from Waimauku.

ABOVE: The other attraction – cool walks in filtered sunshine.

wanting to come back. The neighbours have been here 30 years. Ken Whiteman has farmed on the corner forever.' He ran the last dairy herd in the area and dairying here died the day he retired.

However, not many young people are getting into growing. Partly it's the cost of land. Partly the demands of the job. 'It's hard living off the land, even if you are organised – and we've got a fair whack of labour,' says Joan. 'When you sell, there is only the capital gain on the land. I think it is the same the world over.'

A kilometre or so away is another Altorf block with an orchard and iris fields, run by son Paul. At the bottom of the property is a 3.5-ha artificial lake fed by natural springs and owned by the Rewiti Water Society – a group of neighbouring agriculturists. The 17-m-deep irrigation lake, the biggest in Rodney District when it was dammed in the 1970s, is marked on firefighting maps. In the event of a forest inferno, helicopters with monsoon buckets are likely to descend on the Altorfs without warning.

What takes 32 ha of land, 300 horses and 40,000 people and is just as good at selling a car as a custard square? Answer: the Kumeu Show, the southern hemisphere's biggest one-day **A & P** event.

THAT'S SHOWBIZ
Kumeu Show

Spectators, miniature cattle maybe, participants and all the fun of the fair. Throw in a few stalls, candy floss, a scorcher of a day and . . .

THE KUMEU SHOW IS HELD EACH AUTUMN in the ample Kumeu Showgrounds, where some 500 stalls offer everything from tractors and trucks to hats and tapestries. Visitors can take in woodchopping and shearing contests and dog trials, watch horses put through their paces and bulls strut their stuff, contemplate prize pigs or buy a piece of pottery – all the while discovering endless ways to satisfy their hunger.

Begun way back in 1921, the Kumeu Show has been going ever since, pausing for breath only during the Depression – when it briefly became a sports meet – and in the Second World War.

A perennial favourite in the events calendar, it attracts exhibitors, traders, contestants and spectators from Taupo and beyond, as well as loyal locals. Some families have been rolling up for three and four generations, proving the old adage – there's no business like it.

. . . some healthy competition, including the quest for the district's biggest pumpkin and the gruntiest axeman, and we have a show.

Kumeu is wine country, home to some of the major names in New Zealand's flourishing wine industry. And none is more conspicuous than the House of Nobilo, whose vines march up the hill alongside State Highway 16.

BELOW: Rows of vines and rows of barrels, the former protected from birdstrike by shrouds of fine netting, the latter awaiting the bottling process. Coopers Creek vineyard.

LEFT: The Big Five of the Kumeu district —
Matua Valley, Nobilo, Kumeu River, Coopers Creek and Selak.

BELOW: A taste for the good life? At Coopers Creek
just drop in and find out.

On the other side of Highway 16, past a delightful old dairy factory – built in 1909, and now an attractive restaurant – is Matua Valley Wines. Beyond the white fences, a drive leads up through landscaped grounds to buildings sitting on a rise which overlooks the Waikoukou Valley and rows of tended vines.

Here, on what was formerly a 40-ha dairy farm, brothers Ross and Bill Spence have for more than 22 years been turning out award-winning wines. The country has Ross to thank for recognising the potential of the sauvignon blanc grape that produces wine for which New Zealand has gained a worldwide reputation.

'When we took over the property dairying was in decline,' says Ross. 'Vine planting was too. Corbans was moving from Taupaki and Kumeu and Penfolds had abandoned Waimauku.'

The Spences were undeterred. They felt the place favoured grape growing. The soil was good, and the land lay well to the sun. It was also close to the country's biggest market – Auckland. Problems which made the region expensive for viticulture, such as high humidity and high rainfall, have largely been overcome. Partly, this is the result of new management techniques and concentration on appropriate grape varieties. Partly, it is a change in the weather which, says Ross, has seen drier summers over the past six to seven years. Kumeu, in any case, is helped by being some distance from the Waitakere Ranges, and so has a lower rainfall than Henderson.

Michael Brajkovich, a few kilometres away at Kumeu River Wines, has done his bit to revitalise the district's winemaking reputation. By planting on hillsides to aid drainage, using an improved trellising system and hand-picking grapes, he and his family produced award-winning chardonnays. Michael was the first New Zealander to pass the notoriously difficult London-administered Master of Wine examination.

Michael's father, Dalmatian-born Mate, and his grandfather, bought the property in 1944 from fellow countrymen who for several decades had been tending vines there. In the 1950s it became well-known in Auckland, largely due to the Brajkovich hospitality which saw people such as poets Rex Fairburn and Denis Glover frequent visitors. It is fitting that this winery, which makes wine almost entirely from grapes grown on-site, should be at the forefront of a wine revival in the area.

Most wineries in the rolling countryside around Waimauku and the merging settlements of Huapai and Kumeu are small family affairs. The most obvious exceptions are Matua Valley Wines which produces some 150,000 cases a year, and the House of Nobilo, whose towering cluster of stainless steel vats is a recognisable landmark in Huapai.

TOP: One hot air balloon that seems to know where it's heading.

ABOVE: Waimauku's old dairy ceased operation in 1956. It has since been used for building fibre-glass boats, storing aircraft parts and as a craft shop. It has been a restaurant since 1991.

This old Taupaki homestead will just make the new millennium, but that's about all.

ABOVE: Waimauku to Kumeu is not all flowers and grapes. Here, in Huapai, the Beveridge household tend their hydroponic lettuces seven days a week.

The story of winemaking in Kumeu is like one of those pictures that often decorated the first letter of an illuminated manuscript, bestowing a little charm while hinting at what is to come. There is no liquid refreshment distilled from the land more stylish than wine, and there are few other products with which New Zealand has so spectacularly made its mark internationally.

Imagine, then, the first letter of this chapter decorated with vines, tended by Ross and Bill Spence, and Michael Brajkovich and David Hoskins up in Matakana and all the others in the District who bring to the art of winemaking their passion and skill. Alongside them, in the picture, are the artists and entrepreneurs, the farmers, fishers and beekeepers, the roadmakers, quarriers, guides and conservationists and the host of others who people the land. Further back are the pioneering Europeans and the Maori tribes, the Tangata Whenua, doing what they can — sometimes well, other times badly — to make a life for themselves and their descendants between these disparate coasts.

The next chapter will be written
in a new millennium by new hands;
its picture something we can only imagine.
But there are two things it will show:
the timeless beauty of the place,
and the history of those who called it home.

INDEX

Page numbers in italics refer to photographs

ACKNOWLEDGEMENTS

The publishers are grateful to all the following contributors.
The abbreviations refer to the captions, which in turn identify the photographs:
a = above; *al* = above left; *ar* = above right; *b* = below; *bl* = below left; *br* = below right;
bt = bottom; *l* = left; *fl* = far left; *m* = middle; *r* = right; *t* = top; *tl* = top left; *tr* = top right

Air Logistics 103
Albertland & District Museum 82*l*, 83*b*, 91*t*, 93 *both insets*, 95*t*
Ashmore, M 124*b*
Auckland Art Gallery 37*r*
Auckland Institute & Museum 121*ml*, 123*a*
Auckland Public Library 24*t and a*, 61*t*, 104 *both insets*, 105 *inset*
Auckland Regional Council 8, 76 *all*, 36–37, 68, 69*l*
Albany Studios 43*l*, 141*br*
Beattie, P 1*m*, 6–7, 10, 11, 14*bt*, 15 *all except bl*, 17*fl*, 18, 21*l and
    r*, 23*b*, 25*a and l*, p 28–29, 28*ab and ar*, 29*al*, 30 *both*, 31*bt*,
    32, 33, 37*l*, 38 *both*, 39*t and b*, 40*a*, 41*a*, 42*t*, 43*a*, 44–45, 46*l
    and b*, 47*l*, 48*b*, 49 *all*, 51*l*, 52 *all*, 53 *all except t*, 56*t*, 58 *all*,
    61*m*, 62–63 *all*, 64–65 *all*, 66–67 *all*, 69*bt*, 70 *inset r*, 72*a*, 73
    all, 75*l*, 79*l*, 81 *both*, 82*a*, 83*l*, 84*bt*, 85*m and a*, 86 *both*, 89*l
    and fl*, 92–93, 94 *all*, 106*tl*, 107*l and b*, 110*t, bl and br*, 112
    inset, 113*t*, 119*l*, 125*br*, 138*bl and br*, 139*bl*
Carter Holt Harvey 122 *inset*, 123*l*
Chambers, R 91*l and a*
Department of Conservation 19*r*, 61*r*
Enderby, J & T 2, 3*bl*, 54–55, 74–75*b*, 76–77 *all*
Enzler, R 17*t*
Fotopacific 29*ar*
Godfrey, J / Mainline Steam Trust 109*t*
Greenwood. P 57*al*
Helensville & District Historical Society 100*b*, 101 *all*, 102, 107*bt*,
    111*b*

Howden, C 27*l*, 83*bt*, 85*t*,
Kelly, E & J 1*r*, 13*bt*, 17*a*, 23*a*, 25*b*, 51*al*, 53*t*, 57*t and l*,
MacNut Macadamia Farm 116*t*
Moon, G 3*r*, 18 *inset*, 19 *all except r*
Northern Civil Consulting/Transit NZ [ALPURT] 13*l*
O'Brien, C 7 *(map)* 95*m*, 122*b*, 125*btl*, 140*a*, 141*a*
Puhoi Museum 31*t*, 34*t and a*, 36*fl*, 39*a*, 111*a*
Rodney District Council 35*b*, 48*a*
Rodney Times 36*l*, 42*b*, 84*a and b*
Scott, T 1 *background and bl*, 3 *background and m*,
    4–5, 17*l*, 21*a and inset*, 34–35, 40*m*, 41*t*, 47*r*, 55*b*, 56–57, 59*t*,
    60, 68–69, 69*b*, 70–71, 70 *inset l*, 71 *both insets*, 96–97 *both*,
    98–99 *all*, 100*t and a*, 105*l*, 106*a*, 107*l*, 108*a, r and br*, 110*m*,
    112*b*, 113*a*, 114, 115, 117 *both*, 119*b*, 121*l, inset and a*, 122*t*,
    124*t*, 125*t, m and fungi*, 126 *both a*, 127*b*, 129, 131*l, inset and
    b*, 132, 133 *both*, 124*b and bt*, 135 *both*, 136–7 *all*, 138–9,
    140*t*, 141*t*, 142 *both*
Smart, C 130*bt*
Taylor, T 121*fl, ml and l*, 123*a*
Valentino, R 13*b*, 26 *all*, 34*a*
Vaughan Yarwood 46*r*, 50–51, 72*t*, 75*fl and a*, 79*b*, 89*t and a*,
    95*a*, 110*l*, 116*a*, 121*b*, 127*l and a*, 128*l*, 134*a*
Wainui Historical Society 14*b*, 27 *all except l*, 31*m*, 40*a*, 42*a*, 48*l*
Warkworth & District Museum 12*t*, 34*l*, 44 *inset*, 50*bl and b*
Winstone Aggregates 32 *all*